THE
PILLSBURY
Party
COOKBOOK

Celebration Cake, page 93

THE PILLSBURY

Party

COOKBOOK

DOUBLEDAY

New York   London   Toronto   Sydney   Auckland

The Pillsbury Company
Pillsbury Publications

Publisher: Sally Peters
Managing Editor: Diane B. Anderson
Recipe Copy Editor: Nancy A. Lilleberg
Home Economists: Pillsbury Publications and Consumer Service
Nutrition Coordinators: Patricia Godfrey, R.D., Diane Christensen
Contributing Editor: Heather Randall King
Art Direction and Design: Tad Ware & Company, Inc.
Photography: Studio 3
Food Stylists: JoAnn Cherry, Bonnie Ellingboe, Sharon Harding
Assistant Food Stylist: Mary Margaret Ness
Book Editor: Karen Van Westering
Front Cover Photograph: Pictured clockwise from left: Picadillo Dip
   with tortilla chips, page 37; Green and White Bean Salad, page 38;
   Empanadas, page 37
BinB®, Pillsbury's BEST®, Hungry Jack®, Green Giant®, Harvest Fresh®,
   Niblet Ears®, Rice Originals®, Joan of Arc®, Pillsbury Plus®, Fun-
   fetti®, Princella®, Mexicorn®, Frosting Supreme™ and Valley Combi-
   nations® are registered trademarks of The Pillsbury Company.

PUBLISHED BY DOUBLEDAY
a division of Bantam Doubleday Dell Publishing Group, Inc.
666 Fifth Avenue, New York, New York 10103
DOUBLEDAY and the portrayal of an anchor with a dolphin are trade-
   marks of Doubleday, a division of Bantam Doubleday Dell Publishing
   Group, Inc.
Library of Congress Cataloging-in-Publication Data
The Pillsbury party cookbook.
       p.   cm.
   Includes index.
   1. Holiday cookery.   I. Pillsbury Company.
TX739.P55   1991
641.5′68—dc20   90-47932
                                           CIP

ISBN 0-385-23870-3
Copyright © 1991 by The Pillsbury Company,
Minneapolis, Minnesota
All Rights Reserved
Printed in the United States of America

10   9   8   7   6   5   4   3   2

CONTENTS

Entertaining with Enthusiasm

Entertaining
with
Enthusiasm

*O*ptions for successful entertaining, from grand buffets to simple suppers, are almost endless, and hosts today feel free to showcase their own personal preferences, talents, and styles. The tremendous variety of foods available year-round provides almost unlimited possibilities in planning and choosing a menu. Even the time constraints of the past are lessened by the increased use of convenience appliances that mean hours of preparation are replaced by minutes, even seconds, of streamlined methods.

Although this party potpourri offers complete menus and timetables for a minimum of fuss and worry, we encourage you to mix and match recipes to create your own unique presentations that suit your tastes and needs.

Party Planning Pointers

Planning a party can be as enjoyable as the party itself, if the planning and preparation are done in an organized, stress-free fashion. The key is to start your planning early enough so you don't feel rushed. Equally important is to be realistic when deciding what kind of party to have. Do only what you can handle confidently and comfortably in terms of number of guests, theme, menu, cost and type of service (i.e., sit-down or buffet). Remember to keep in mind the amount of space you have—both in the kitchen for food preparation and in the living area for serving and eating.

List-making is the secret to success for any party, and for a larger one it becomes an absolute essential. From the moment you decide to have a party, begin to make lists:
• a schedule of what needs to be done when
• a guest list, and eventually the acceptances and regrets
• items to be purchased: food, beverages, paper goods, decorations, favors
• equipment you may need to rent or borrow: chairs, card tables, serving pieces, coffee maker, linens, glassware, etc.

Other Helpful Suggestions

• Do any cleaning, washing and polishing tasks well in advance.
• Place special food or equipment orders and hire serving and clean-up help in advance.
• Whatever size group you are entertaining, provide an adequate supply of guest towels, coat hangers, ash trays, chairs and other amenities.
• Unless you live in Camelot, never depend on the weather to cooperate for an outdoor party. Have an alternative plan to move inside or gather on the following day.
• If children are accompanying adults, arrange a special play area for them, complete with games and toys. Engage a child-care person, if necessary, to keep them entertained so parents are free to enjoy the party.

Creating the Atmosphere

Although the focal point of much of our entertaining today is the food, choosing a theme and coordinating the various elements, from the menu to the decorations, can turn even a small, simple occasion into a festive party. Often the reason for having a gathering readily suggests a theme. A bon voyage party for friends traveling to the Caribbean offers a perfect opportunity to serve a Creole-inspired menu and to decorate with tropical flowers. Birthday parties are another opportunity to dress up the occasion with a theme appropriate to the interests of the celebrant, be it gardening, baseball, dinosaurs or the movies.

The advantage of organizing your party around a theme is that it gives you a reason to coordinate all aspects of the party—the food, invitations, decorations, party favors, perhaps even the background music and the dress. However, let common sense be your guide and don't allow the special theme to overwhelm your planning. After all, the guests and the food are what make a party truly memorable.

Invitations: The tone or atmosphere of the party can begin with the invitations. Although guests can be easily invited by telephone or face-to-face, a written invitation does more to set the stage for an event. Whether invitations are store-bought or specially designed and printed to reflect the party theme, guests appreciate having in hand all the necessary information—hosts, date, location, time, theme, appropriate dress and any other particulars that make the event special. Particularly for a large gathering it is useful to include complete directions to the party site and any parking instructions, plus daytime and evening numbers for acceptances and regrets.

Invitations should be mailed two to three weeks in advance of the party and four weeks ahead for a wedding reception or especially large event. They should go to all guests on the same day whenever possible so no one feels like a substitute for another who couldn't come.

Telephoned invitations are appropriate when the gathering is spur-of-the-moment, the theme casual, when close friends are the invitees and when the hostess needs an immediate reply. A reminder call frequently is necessary with face-to-face or telephone invitations, particularly when the prospective guest is not in a position to write down necessary details or respond without further checking.

Guests should be courteous and respond promptly to the invitation so plans can proceed accordingly. In the acceptance, hosts should confirm essentials like date and time to avoid embarrassing misunderstandings.

Centerpieces: Although floral arrangements are traditional centerpieces, you can vary the usual with any number of colorful, attractive substitutes. A spectacular fresh fruit and vegetable arrangement reminiscent of Williamsburg styling can double as centerpiece and part of a fruit and cheese dessert. Or, if dessert is a spectacular cake, it too can serve double duty as focal point and grand finale for your celebration. Dried flowers, a silk arrangement you usually place elsewhere in your home, a dewy-fresh, just-picked garden bouquet or one perfect flower at each place can be enchanting and economical. Other suggestions? Small decorative pots of herbs, collections of shells, decorated eggs, a basket of gourmet candies, dramatic paper flowers in vivid colors, candle groupings or a spotlessly clean fishbowl complete with lively residents and colored marbles. The key is choosing a centerpiece that complements the theme and color scheme and contributes to a memorable occasion.

Planning the Menu

Deciding on a menu involves some common sense as well as your preferences in food. Carefully consider your personal cooking skills and the time you will have available to prepare the food. Be realistic and don't try to do more than you know you can manage. A consideration often overlooked is the amount of cold storage and oven space you will have available. Nothing can be more frustrating than to have the cooking under way and find there is no more room. If you are planning a buffet, choose foods that can be easily managed with a fork and are sans soupy sauces and drippy marinades. No food should be so delicate that it will wilt, melt or fall before the last person in line has been served.

Economize by creating a menu that incorporates foods that are in season at the time of your party. Such foods are usually less expensive and of better quality. Select foods that can be prepared at spaced intervals—not all the day before or day of the party. The Preparation Timetables included with each of the menus in this book can assist in this planning. Items like ice rings for punch, breads and many desserts can be prepared weeks, even months in advance. Consult the Guide for Freezing Baked Foods for optimum storage times and be sure each item is suitably wrapped in moisture- and vapor-proof materials that are airtight. We recommend leaving frosting and other decorating steps for close to serving time after frozen foods have been thawed.

If you intend to serve wines or mixed drinks during a cocktail hour and/or throughout the evening, have plenty of glasses, cocktail napkins, ice and garnishes (citrus wedges and twists, olives, etc.) set out at an easily reached serving place away from the food. Hire a bartender for a large group. And for a smaller group encourage your guests to serve themselves. Punches can be festive and more economical. Offer nonalcoholic as well as alcoholic beverages and use ice rings or molds rather than cubes to keep mixtures well chilled and less diluted.

Quantity Planning Guide For Fresh Fruits, Vegetables, Chips, Crackers and Punch

FRUITS: Allow ½ cup per serving.

18 pounds watermelon
(bite-sized chunks) . . . . 16 cups
4 pounds pineapple
(bite-sized chunks) . . . . 5 cups
3 pounds honeydew or cantaloupe
(bite-sized chunks) . . . . 4 cups
1 pint strawberries, blueberries or
raspberries . . . . 2 cups
1 pound grapes . . . . .2 to 3 cups
3 ounces kiwifruit . . . . ½ cup

VEGETABLES: Allow 4 to 6 pieces per serving.

2 pounds broccoli or
cauliflower . . . . 32 (1¼-inch) florets
1 pound carrots . . . . . . 65 (3 × ½-inch) sticks
1¾ pounds celery . . . . 100 (4 × ½-inch) sticks
1 pint cherry tomatoes   25 (1-inch) tomatoes
1½ pounds cucumber . . . . . 50 (¼-inch) slices
1 pound zucchini (2 medium) . . . 50 (¼-inch)
slices

DIPS: Allow 1 tablespoon per serving.

1 cup dip . . . . 16 servings

CHIPS:

1½ pounds . . . . 25 servings

CRACKERS:

¾ to 1 pound . . . . 25 servings

PUNCH: Allow ½ cup per serving.

1 gallon . . . . 30 servings

Innovative Ways with Napkins

Napkins: Various colors, material textures and innovative ways to fold napkins can greatly enhance the visual excitement of a party. Elegant fabrics in pastel shades, white or cream spell formality. In contrast, woven fabrics of vivid hues and colorful paper napkins signal a more informal ambiance. And, of course, there are other options that can complement your theme. Let your imagination flow!

Placement of napkins can be as conventional or dramatic as you wish. Besides the suggestions shown in the illustrations, napkins can be rolled up or gathered into a variety of rings coordinated with other table appointments. They can be tucked into goblets, rolled around flatware and tied with cord or ribbon for a buffet or arranged to the left of the fork or on the plate.

For best results with the folds shown, use starched cloth napkins that have been stored flat. Folds can be done several days or hours before the party. Store readied napkins lightly covered to keep them dust-free. Just follow instructions step by step and see what delightful shapes result.

Although luncheon-sized napkins are appropriate for daytime entertaining and appetizer buffets, the larger, dinner-sized napkins are traditional and more practical for full meals served in the evening.

MEXICAN STYLE

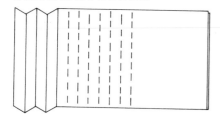 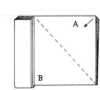 

1. Fold napkin in half. Turn napkin long way and make 1″ pleats in three fourths of napkin.

2. Fold napkin in half again with pleats on outside. Bring all four points at A to B.

3. Set napkin upright on table. Let go of pleats first, then the base.

PINWHEEL

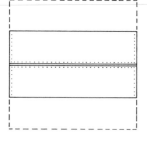 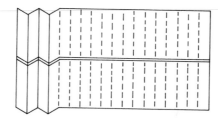 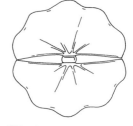

1. Fold napkin's top and bottom edges to center.

2. Fold napkin from left to right in 1-inch accordion pleats.

3. Clip in center with napkin clip or ribbon. Spread out pleats to form pinwheel.

LILY FLOWER

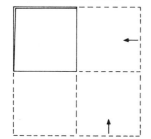 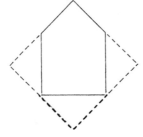 

1. With right side down, fold into quarters; rotate to place points up.

2. Fold back left, right and bottom corners.

3. Pleat softly; even folds to shape. Place in napkin ring.

Napkin Folds

Food Purchasing Guide for Parties

Food Items	Serving Size	25 Servings	50 Servings	100 Servings
Meats, Cheeses and Buns				
Ham, turkey, cold cuts (½ oz. slices)	2 to 3 oz.	3 to 5 lb.	7 to 9 lb.	14 to 18 lb.
Cheese slices (½ oz. slices)	1 to 1½ oz.	1½ to 2½ lb.	3 to 5 lb.	6 to 10 lb.
Buns	1½ buns	3 dozen	6 dozen	12 dozen
Prepared Foods				
Chicken or Potato Salad	½ cup	1 gallon	2 gallons	4 gallons
Condiments				
Mayonnaise	1 to 2 teaspoons	½ to 1 cup	1 to 2 cups	2 to 4 cups
Mustard	1 teaspoon	½ cup	1 cup	2 cups
Olives (small or medium)	2 to 3	6 oz.	1 lb.	2 lb.
Pickles (medium spear)	1	1 quart	2 quarts	4 quarts
Desserts				
Cake	2 × 2-inch piece	¼ sheet cake (24 pcs.)	½ sheet cake (48 pcs.)	1 sheet cake (96 pcs.)
Ice Cream	½ cup	1 gallon	2 gallons	4 gallons
Ice Cream Toppings	2 tablespoons	3 cups	6 cups	12 cups
Mixed Nuts	1½ tablespoons	¼ to ¾ lb.	1 to 1½ lb.	2 to 3 lb.
Mints				
small pillow	1 to 2	¼ to ½ lb.	½ to 1 lb.	1 to 2 lb.
wafer	1	¾ lb.	1½ lb.	3 lb.
Beverages				
Coffee	¾ cup (6 oz)	½ lb.	1 lb.	2 lb.
Coffee Cream	1 teaspoon	½ pint	1 pint	1 quart
Punch	½ cup (4 oz.)	1 gallon	2 gallons	4 gallons
Sugar Cubes	1 cube	6 oz.	¾ lb.	1½ lb.

Shopping Tips

Once a menu is determined, food purchasing is the next step. Begin by reviewing recipe ingredients and make several grocery lists according to when each item can safely be purchased. We suggest dividing your shopping list into three sections:
- items like paper, plastic or nonperishable foods that can be purchased weeks in advance and stored in the pantry
- groceries that can be purchased the week of the party
- highly perishable items like bakery goods, fresh fruits and vegetables, flowers that must be last-minute purchases or special orders which must be picked up

Quality ingredients are essential for quality results. When choosing your food purchases, remember:
- fresh foods should be at their seasonal best and at the peak of flavor, texture and color. If you are harvesting your own fruits and vegetables, do so in the cool morning hours before the hot sun can cause wilting.
- With frozen foods, proper storage should be apparent with no evidence of damaging freezer burn or dryness due to torn packaging.
- Canned foods should be preserved in dent-free containers with no sign of leakage.

Guide for Freezing Baked Foods

	What Can I Freeze	Special Tips for Freezing	Keep	How to Thaw and Serve
Breads	Yeast coffee cakes, muffins and quick breads can be frozen.	Cool completely before freezing. Do not frost or decorate before freezing. Wrap in airtight, moistureproof wrap. Place coffee cakes on foil-wrapped cardboard; then wrap.	2 to 3 months	Unwrap slightly; thaw at room temperature 2 to 3 hours. Serve at room temperature or reheat, wrapped in foil, at 350°F. for about 15 to 20 minutes. Frost and decorate, if desired.
Cakes	Both frosted and unfrosted cakes can be frozen.	Cool completely. Wrap unfrosted cake in airtight, moistureproof wrap. Buttercream frosting freezes best. Allow frosting to harden by placing frosted cake in refrigerator or freezer before wrapping. Place layer cakes in cake containers or bakery boxes to prevent crushing.	Unfrosted—4 to 6 months Frosted—1 to 2 months	Unfrosted—Thaw at room temperature, covered, 3 to 4 hours. Frost or serve according to recipe. Frosted—Thaw, loosely covered, overnight in refrigerator.
Cookies	Baked cookies can be frozen.	Wrap unfrosted cookies in airtight, moisture-proof wrap or place in plastic containers. If frosted or decorated before freezing, first freeze quickly on cookie sheet; then package frozen cookies between layers of waxed paper in rigid container for further freezing.	Unfrosted—4 to 6 months Frosted—1 to 2 months	Thaw in package at room temperature. For cookies that should be crisp when thawed, remove from container.

Food Preparation Tips

Before you begin any of the food preparation, read through each recipe in your menu. Then assemble all ingredients, utensils and cookware to make certain you have everything on hand. Preparation will be easier and results more successful if you avoid substituting ingredients and equipment. Also take care to use the technique (slicing, dicing, shredding, etc.) specified to achieve even cooking and the desired appearance.

Cook's helpers such as the mixer, blender, deep-fat fryer, food processor and microwave can save time and work if used wisely. Be aware of when each can be used to full advantage and when it might be quicker and easier to tackle a job by hand. For efficiency, complete similar tasks when utensils are readily available—i.e., do all necessary dicing, chopping and slicing of foods at the same time.

Other preparation tips

- Be alert to special instructions like heat oven, refrigerate dough, soften butter or cream cheese, grease and flour pans, chill bowl and beaters before whipping cream, marinate, and other directions that take extra time.
- Keep your work space tidy, removing ingredients and utensils after use. Tasks can be accomplished more quickly in an uncluttered, organized environment.
- Think about garnishes as you work. Retaining a few grated carrots to sprinkle over a frosted carrot cake or setting aside some whole nuts to arrange over a salad or dessert can add that final presentation plus without having to purchase extra ingredients.
- If something "fails," don't despair. Just think of another way it can be served. A dessert that doesn't set as firmly as you had hoped, for instance, may look very attractive spooned into pretty individual dishes and garnished with a flourish.
- If time runs out and you have no time to prepare a portion of the meal you had planned to serve, substitute a commercially or deli-prepared item. Potato salad or coleslaw, for example, can be purchased, spooned into an attractive serving bowl and artfully garnished with colorful red and green pepper strips, radish roses, herb sprigs or snow pea pods.

Picnic Pointers

Several of these menus, such as the Memorial Day Picnic or Teddy Bear Picnic, have been created specifically as picnics, and others could easily be served out of doors, whether in your own backyard or at the beach or park. If you do choose to serve these menus, or ones you create yourself, in outdoor settings, care must be given to two special concerns: food safety and packing.

Picnics and sunny, warm days pair perfectly. But these same idyllic conditions we love serve as a lure for uninvited food spoilage bacteria. As a result, we urge you to heed the following tips for toting foods safely, especially in very hot weather or for long distances:

- Foods highly susceptible to spoilage include dairy products, high-protein items and mixtures. Popular picnic items that require chilled toting are macaroni, egg and potato salads, deviled eggs, poultry, meats and fish.

- Safe temperatures for holding foods for a period of time are hot foods at 140°F or above and cold foods at 40°F or below.
- Transport thoroughly chilled foods in an ice chest or other insulated cooler with plenty of ice, or with containers of artificial refrigerant, leaving space for air to circulate.
- Hot foods will retain heat for one to two hours if wrapped immediately upon removal from the oven with several layers of foil and then newspapers.
- Pack thoroughly heated or chilled foods in separate containers.
- Take only as much food as you think you think will be eaten. Do not save leftovers.
- Set coolers out of the sun and open only when necessary.
- Unpack food only when everyone is ready to eat.

Remember that **it is often impossible to detect food spoilage in process.** Bacteria at work over several hours usually do not change the taste, odor or appearance of unrefrigerated foods. And it takes only an hour for bacteria to grow in warm, moist conditions.

Packing Tips

The following practical tips can make portable parties more fun and less work:

- Make a list of items you want to take along— foods, utensils, tableware, cleanup supplies. Check off items as you pack.
- Use sturdy carrying equipment. Strong handles and lids that won't blow away are helpful.
- Choose accessories to suit the occasion and setting. China and glassware are elegant for several adults; paper and plastic are appropriate for larger groups and for children.
- Pack food and nonfood items separately and in the order they will be used.
- Choose thermal and other containers that seal tightly for liquids. Pack upright and brace with surrounding items.
- Label foods that cannot be seen through the wrap or container.
- Bring drinking water if it is not available at the picnic site.
- Tuck in suntan lotion, moist towelettes or wet cloth in a plastic bag, insect repellent, first-aid kit and, if outing is after dark, a flashlight.
- Save foil and plastic wrap to wrap dirty utensils and items to go in the trash. For large gatherings, bring several large trash bags for cleanup in order to leave an area clean.

Buffet Serving Suggestions

In addition to good food, a bountiful buffet offers convenience and flexibility to both hosts and guests. This serve-yourself arrangement encourages guests to mingle, and if space is limited can accommodate more people.

For a small group, a sideboard or tea cart works beautifully for the food presentation. A large rectangular table, set away from a wall so two lines of people can help themselves simultaneously, is perfect for large gatherings like receptions, teas and open houses. In contrast, an attractive, uncluttered kitchen counter or round game table provides a charming serving station for informal gatherings and kids' parties.

Arrange the buffet table with sturdy dinner plates placed at one end of the table or on a nearby sideboard, table or server. Then place the food in a logical progression, moving from hot dishes to cold and grouping together similar dishes such as vegetables, salads, etc. If the entree is to be spooned over pasta or rice, either of those is placed before the entree. All sauces, gravies, condiments and dressings should be close to the dishes they embellish so there is no question about what foods go together. Your goal is to make selection as easy as possible, to avoid lengthy delays in serving and to minimize the amount of juggling guests must do.

Unless guests are to be seated at preset tables after moving through the buffet line, flatware and napkins should be the final items they pick up after filling their plates. Napkins rolled around forks add measurably to serving ease and require little space. Often it is more convenient to set up a beverage station on a separate table, or to pour beverages after guests are settled in their chairs. Desserts can be arranged with after-dinner coffee on a separate table. Or, if they are easily handled, like cookies and bars, they can be placed after breads on the buffet table.

Other tips for streamlining your buffet? Avoid accidental spills by placing serving dishes with enough space between each so that plates can be set down if necessary for filling. Meats should be presliced, breads and rolls buttered and molded salads and desserts already cut into serving-sized pieces.

Serving dishes should be large enough so they don't constantly need refilling. Hot foods can be kept at perfect eating temperature with a little help from warming plates and trays, fondue pots, candle warmers and other heating devices. Chilled foods look festive and remain cold when presented on beds of chipped ice.

The following buffet arrangement is designed to keep serving lines moving comfortably and quickly. It is easily adjusted to suit a variety of table shapes, space considerations and use of tea carts or side tables for additional courses.

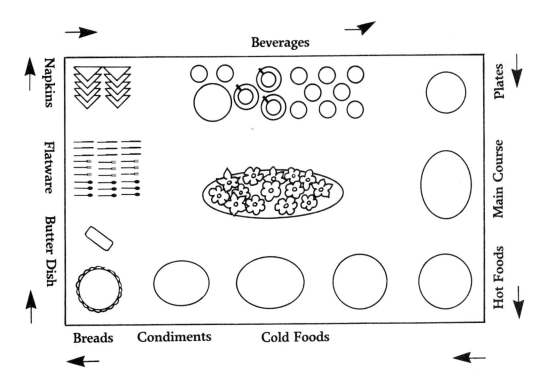

Graduation Tostada Buffet, page 22

Life's Special Celebrations

*L*ife's milestones—graduations, weddings, showers, retirements, housewarmings, anniversaries and others are meant to be shared. No better way than with a get-together, formal or informal, to mark each occasion and add your own best wishes in a significantly personal way.

Most successful hosts agree that entertaining is easier and more fun, as well as more interesting for everyone involved, if there is a theme. These special celebrations provide just that—a reason for throwing a party and a logical starting place for planning invitations, decorations, music, gifts etc. Guests usually respond enthusiastically by going all out to make the event a "happening," whether it is keeping the party a secret, dressing in special clothes, contributing to the meal or participating in the evening's entertainment.

This section provides many ideas to stimulate your imagination for making the most of whatever milestone is being celebrated. We hope that you will be inspired to honor someone close to you with such a special celebration. Many of the menus lend themselves beautifully to cooperative efforts so that if you need extra help, it can be easily achieved. On the other hand, if you choose to handle all the preparation on your own, you will not be overwhelmed by having to research recipes, guess at timings and then wonder if foods will taste and look good. All these details are organized for you by our skilled home economists who are busy people too, but who still take great pleasure in marking life's special celebrations in unique, memorable ways.

Pictured clockwise from top left: Pitter-Patter Petits Fours, page 21; Mini Lemon Nutmeg Muffins, page 20; Ham and Cheese Roll-Ups with Fruit Platter, page 20

Pitter-Patter Baby Shower

Serves 12
Lemonade
Mini Lemon Nutmeg Muffins*
Ham and Cheese Roll-Ups with Fruit Platter*
Salmon Tea Triangles*
Pitter-Patter Petits Fours*
Nuts   Mints
Coffee   Tea
*Recipe included

Weeks before the "pitter-patter of little feet" becomes a reality, surprise the parents-to-be with a shower featuring a baby buggy full of infant needs. Or use a baby bathtub or diaper pail to hold the gifts and then send it home with the guests of honor.

Opportunities for creativity at such a special time are endless, and planning the menu is no exception. The one that follows is versatile enough for a luncheon, tea or light supper; the selections lend themselves to simple buffet serving and plate-on-the-lap dining. Quick-to-make Mini Lemon Nutmeg Muffins and the adorable Pitter-Patter Petits Fours begin with mixes and end with many compliments for the cook.

For a centerpiece, consider a basket decorated as a baby buggy, small plush animals in soft colors or baby's breath combined with other fresh flowers and festooned with satin ribbon. Paper bibs make creative place mats if you are setting tables. And napkins folded like diapers and secured with diaper pins are certain to invite smiles and conversation.

You will want to record this cherished event, so invite someone to capture the shower on film or video. After baby arrives and you pay a welcoming visit, take along a special album containing the party photographs. Your thoughtfulness will be remembered for years to come by both parents and child.

Preparation Timetable

Day of Shower

Early in the Day: Prepare *Pitter-Patter Petits Fours;* cover loosely and store at room temperature.

Several Hours Before: Prepare *Ham and Cheese Roll-Ups with Fruit Platter* and *Salmon Tea Triangles;* cover and refrigerate • Prepare lemonade.

Shortly Before Serving: Place nuts and mints in serving bowls • Prepare *Mini Lemon Nutmeg Muffins* • Prepare coffee and/or tea.

Mini Lemon Nutmeg Muffins

MUFFINS
1 package nut or date bread mix*
1 cup milk
⅓ cup oil*
1 egg
1 teaspoon grated lemon peel
½ teaspoon nutmeg

GLAZE
½ cup sugar
1 tablespoon lemon juice
1 tablespoon water
¼ teaspoon almond extract

Heat oven to 375° F. Generously grease bottoms only of 44 miniature muffin cups or line with miniature paper baking cups. In large bowl, combine all muffin ingredients; stir 50 to 75 strokes until dry particles are moistened. Fill greased muffin cups ⅔ full. Bake at 375° F. for 10 to 15 minutes or until toothpick inserted in center comes out clean. Cool 5 minutes; remove from pan.

In small bowl, combine all glaze ingredients until well blended. Drizzle glaze over warm muffins. **44 mini muffins.**

TIPS: *If using date bread mix, decrease oil to ¼ cup. Bake as directed above.

To prepare regular muffins, grease 12 muffin cups or line with paper baking cups. Bake at 375° F. for 20 to 25 minutes.

HIGH ALTITUDE—Above 3500 Feet: Add 2 tablespoons flour to dry bread mix. Bake as directed above.

NUTRITION INFORMATION PER SERVING

SERVING SIZE: 1 MINI MUFFIN		PERCENT U.S. RDA PER SERVING	
Calories	70	Protein	*
Protein	1 g	Vitamin A	*
Carbohydrate	10 g	Vitamin C	*
Fat	3 g	Thiamine	2%
Cholesterol	5 mg	Riboflavin	2%
Sodium	45 mg	Niacin	*
Potassium	25 mg	Calcium	*
		Iron	*

*Contains less than 2% of the U.S. RDA of this nutrient.

Salmon Tea Triangles

Butter or margarine
6 thin slices whole wheat sandwich bread, crusts removed
1 (7½-ounce) can salmon, drained
1 (3-ounce) package cream cheese, softened
¼ cup finely chopped seeded cucumber
2 tablespoons finely chopped celery
2 tablespoons finely chopped green onions
Cucumber slices
Fresh dill weed

Spread butter on 1 side of each bread slice. In small bowl, combine salmon, cream cheese, ¼ cup cucumber, celery and onions; mix well. Spread about ¼ cup salmon mixture on buttered side of each bread slice. Cut sandwiches diagonally into 4 triangles. Garnish sandwiches with cucumber slices and dill weed. Cover; refrigerate 1 to 2 hours before serving. **24 triangles.**

NUTRITION INFORMATION PER SERVING

SERVING SIZE: 1 TRIANGLE		PERCENT U.S. RDA PER SERVING	
Calories	40	Protein	2%
Protein	2 g	Vitamin A	2%
Carbohydrate	2 g	Vitamin C	2%
Fat	3 g	Thiamine	*
Cholesterol	10 mg	Riboflavin	*
Sodium	75 mg	Niacin	2%
Potassium	60 mg	Calcium	2%
		Iron	*

*Contains less than 2% of the U.S. RDA of this nutrient.

Ham and Cheese Roll-Ups with Fruit Platter

ROLL-UPS
2 (3-ounce) packages cream cheese, softened
¼ cup dairy sour cream
1 tablespoon Dijon mustard
24 (4 × 4-inch) thin slices cooked ham

FRUIT PLATTER
Select 3 or 4 of the following:
1 pint (2 cups) fresh strawberries
2 kiwifruit, peeled, sliced
1 cantaloupe, seeded, peeled, cut into thin wedges
1 pound seedless red or green grapes, separated into clusters
1 small pineapple, cored, peeled, cut into bite-sized pieces

In a small bowl, combine cream cheese, sour cream and mustard; blend until smooth. Spread about 2 teaspoons cheese filling evenly on each ham slice; roll up. Arrange ham rolls (seam side down) and selected fruits on platter. Cover; refrigerate several hours before serving. **24 Roll-Ups.**

NUTRITION INFORMATION PER SERVING

SERVING SIZE: 1 ROLL-UP EXCLUDING FRUIT		PERCENT U.S. RDA PER SERVING	
Calories	60	Protein	6%
Protein	4 g	Vitamin A	2%
Carbohydrate	1 g	Vitamin C	4%
Fat	4 g	Thiamine	6%
Cholesterol	16 mg	Riboflavin	2%
Sodium	210 mg	Niacin	2%
Potassium	55 mg	Calcium	*
		Iron	*

*Contains less than 2% of the U.S. RDA of this nutrient.

Pitter-Patter Petits Fours

1 package pudding-included white cake mix
1¼ cups water
¼ cup oil
3 egg whites
2 tablespoons Amaretto, if desired
3 cups powdered sugar
¼ cup water
3 tablespoons light corn syrup
2 tablespoons margarine or butter, melted
½ teaspoon vanilla
¼ teaspoon almond extract
Frosting tinted pink and blue
Decorating bag and tips

Heat oven to 350° F. Grease and flour 15 × 10 × 1-inch baking pan. In large bowl combine cake mix, 1¼ cups water, oil and egg whites at low speed until moistened; beat 2 minutes at high speed. Pour batter into greased and floured pan. Bake at 350° F. for 20 to 30 minutes or until toothpick inserted in center comes out clean; cool.

Brush top of cake with Amaretto. To avoid cake crumbs, freeze cake 1 hour before cutting. Cut cake into pieces using foot-shaped and/or 2-inch round cookie cutters.* Set cake pieces on wire rack over waxed paper.

In small bowl, combine powdered sugar, ¼ cup water, corn syrup, margarine, vanilla and almond extract at low speed until powdered sugar is moistened; beat at high speed until smooth. If necessary, add 2 to 3 teaspoons water until icing is of desired consistency. Spoon icing evenly over top and sides of cake pieces. (Icing that drips off can be reused.) Using tinted frosting, outline and decorate foot-shaped petits fours; outline and decorate round petits fours to resemble baby bibs. **20 to 24 petits fours.**

TIP: *To cut out foot-shaped cakes without a cookie cutter, trace pattern piece provided and cut from heavy paper or light cardboard; place pattern on cake and cut around it with a sharp knife.

HIGH ALTITUDE—Above 3500 Feet: Add ½ cup flour to dry cake mix and increase water to 1¾ cups. Bake as directed above.

NUTRITION INFORMATION PER SERVING			
SERVING SIZE: 1 PETIT FOUR		PERCENT U.S. RDA PER SERVING	
Calories	190	Protein	2%
Protein	1 g	Vitamin A	*
Carbohydrate	34 g	Vitamin C	*
Fat	6 g	Thiamine	2%
Cholesterol	0 mg	Riboflavin	2%
Sodium	150 mg	Niacin	2%
Potassium	15 mg	Calcium	4%
		Iron	2%

*Contains less than 2% of the U.S. RDA of this nutrient.

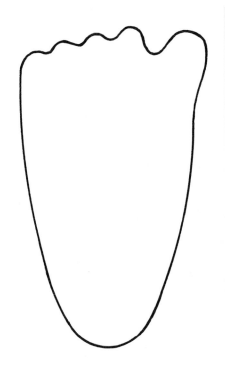

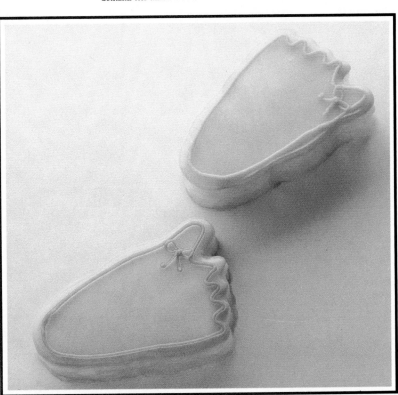

Pitter-Patter Petits Fours

Pictured top to bottom: Refried Beans; Orange-Melon Salad, page 24; Tostadas, page 25

Graduation Tostada Buffet

Serves 12
Grape Juice and Fruit Sangria*
Orange-Melon Salad*
Mexicorn® Relish* Tostadas*
Refried Beans
Salsa* Guacamole*
Sour Cream   Sliced Ripe Olives,
Shredded Monterey Jack and Cheddar Cheese
Choffee Chiffon Cake*

*Recipe included

With "Pomp and Circumstance" in the past and diplomas in hand, the graduates are ready to celebrate! A fiesta motif with bold flavors and flamboyant colors mirrors that "We made it!" mood in superb style. You can count on your guests to provide hearty appetites, a zest for Tex-Mex cuisine and an appreciation of the casual scene.

Appropriate for a patio, deck or porch setting, the festive fare is easily arranged on one or more picnic tables. Use your brightest cloths or mats and place foods in an order for easy assembling. Begin with dinner plates and follow with the tortillas, refried beans, beef and chicken fillings, chopped and shredded items, salsa, sour cream and guacamole toppings and finally, the sensational salad. This fruit combo, a refreshing counterpoint to the assertive flavors of spicy foods, should be served with a slotted spoon. Or provide small bowls to catch the juices.

To avoid crowding, have plenty of chilled beverages on another table away from the food where guests can help themselves throughout the party. For a more elaborate dessert, enhance the Choffee Chiffon Cake with a make-your-own sundae bar. Just prefreeze chocolate, coffee and vanilla ice cream balls and offer a variety of toppings—flavored syrups, marshmallow creme, salted nuts, whipped cream, etc.

Another plus, almost every recipe can be readied ahead and refrigerated until serving or reheating time.

Preparation Timetable

Several Days Ahead

Bake *Choffee Chiffon Cake* but do not slice into layers and frost; cool completely, wrap and freeze • Prepare *Mexicorn® Relish* and *Salsa;* cover and refrigerate.

Day Before Buffet

Refrigerate juice and carbonated beverage for *Grape Juice and Fruit Sangria* • Prepare beef filling for *Tostadas;* cover and refrigerate.

Day of Buffet

Early in the Day: Remove cake from freezer to thaw • Shred lettuce and chop tomatoes for tostadas; shred cheeses. Place in serving bowls; cover and refrigerate • Place sour cream and olives in serving bowls; cover and refrigerate.

Several Hours Before: Prepare *Orange-Melon Salad* and *Guacamole;* cover and refrigerate • Prepare frosting and assemble cake.

Shortly Before Serving: Prepare sangria • Arrange all tostada toppings on serving table • Heat refried beans and beef fillings for tostadas; place in serving bowls and keep warm • Fry tortillas for tostadas.

Grape Juice and Fruit Sangria

2 quarts (8 cups) grape juice
2 lemons, sliced
4 limes, cut into wedges
2 oranges, thinly sliced, slices halved
2½ cups lemon-lime-flavored carbonated
     beverage, chilled
4 cups ice cubes

In 3-quart nonmetal container, combine grape juice and fruit, slightly squeezing lemon, lime and orange slices into juice mixture. Refrigerate until thoroughly chilled. Just before serving, pour mixture into punch bowl; add carbonated beverage and ice cubes, stirring to combine.
12 (1-cup) servings.

NUTRITION INFORMATION: Variables in this recipe make it impossible to calculate nutrition information.

Orange-Melon Salad

1 honeydew melon, cut into cubes or balls
6 oranges, peeled, cut up
1 (6-ounce) can frozen limeade concentrate,
    thawed

In large bowl, combine all ingredients. Cover; refrigerate 1 to 2 hours. Garnish as desired.
12 to 14 servings.

NUTRITION INFORMATION PER SERVING
SERVING SIZE: 1/14 OF RECIPE

Calories	90	Protein	*
Protein	1 g	Vitamin A	2%
Carbohydrate	23 g	Vitamin C	90%
Fat	0 g	Thiamine	8%
Cholesterol	0 mg	Riboflavin	2%
Sodium	10 mg	Niacin	2%
Potassium	360 mg	Calcium	2%
		Iron	*

*Contains less than 2% of the U.S. RDA of this nutrient.

Mexicorn® Relish

¼ cup sugar
1 teaspoon instant minced onion
½ teaspoon dry mustard
½ teaspoon celery seed
¼ cup cider vinegar
1 (11-ounce) can vacuum-packed whole kernel
    corn with sweet peppers, drained

In small saucepan, combine sugar, onion, mustard, celery seed and vinegar; bring to a boil. Stir in corn; simmer 10 minutes. Place in bowl; cover and refrigerate 8 to 10 hours or overnight.
1¾ cups.

NUTRITION INFORMATION PER SERVING
SERVING SIZE: 1 TABLESPOON

Calories	16	Protein	*
Protein	0 g	Vitamin A	*
Carbohydrate	4 g	Vitamin C	*
Fat	0 g	Thiamine	*
Cholesterol	0 mg	Riboflavin	*
Sodium	30 mg	Niacin	*
Potassium	25 mg	Calcium	*
		Iron	*

*Contains less than 2% of the U.S. RDA of this nutrient.

Salsa

1 (28-ounce) can (3 cups) tomato wedges or
    whole tomatoes, drained, chopped*
1 (4-ounce) can chopped green chiles**
½ cup thinly sliced green onions
1 teaspoon grated lemon peel, if desired
½ teaspoon salt
½ teaspoon dried oregano leaves
⅛ teaspoon pepper
2 to 3 tablespoons lemon juice
2 tablespoons oil

In large bowl, combine all ingredients; mix well. Cover; refrigerate several hours to blend flavors.
2½ cups.

TIPS: *Two cups (2 to 3 medium) chopped peeled fresh tomatoes can be substituted for canned tomatoes.

**One to 2 fresh jalapeño chiles, seeded and finely chopped, can be substituted for canned chiles.

NUTRITION INFORMATION PER SERVING
SERVING SIZE: 1 TABLESPOON

Calories	12	Protein	*
Protein	0 g	Vitamin A	8%
Carbohydrate	1 g	Vitamin C	8%
Fat	1 g	Thiamine	*
Cholesterol	0 mg	Riboflavin	*
Sodium	60 mg	Niacin	*
Potassium	50 mg	Calcium	*
		Iron	*

*Contains less than 2% of the U.S. RDA of this nutrient.

Guacamole

2 large ripe avocados, halved, peeled
¼ cup mayonnaise or salad dressing
1 to 3 tablespoons lemon juice
5 to 8 drops hot pepper sauce
¼ teaspoon salt
Dash pepper

In small bowl, mash avocados. Add remaining ingredients; blend well. Cover; refrigerate 1 to 2 hours to blend flavors.
1½ cups.

NUTRITION INFORMATION PER SERVING
SERVING SIZE: 1 TABLESPOON

Calories	45	Protein	*
Protein	0 g	Vitamin A	2%
Carbohydrate	1 g	Vitamin C	2%
Fat	4 g	Thiamine	*
Cholesterol	1 mg	Riboflavin	*
Sodium	35 mg	Niacin	*
Potassium	105 mg	Calcium	*
		Iron	*

*Contains less than 2% of the U.S. RDA of this nutrient.

Tostadas

3 pounds ground beef
1 cup chopped onion
2 (16-ounce) cans (4 cups) tomatoes,
    undrained, cut up
2 (8-ounce) cans (2 cups) tomato sauce
2 teaspoons salt
2 to 6 teaspoons chili powder
1 teaspoon dried oregano leaves
½ teaspoon cumin
½ cup oil
16 (8-inch) flour tortillas
    Refried beans
    Shredded lettuce
    Chopped tomatoes
    Guacamole
    Salsa

In a Dutch oven, brown ground beef and onion;
drain. Add tomatoes, tomato sauce, salt, chili
powder, oregano leaves and cumin; mix well.
Simmer 25 to 30 minutes, stirring occasionally,
until thoroughly heated and flavors are well
blended.

In 10-inch skillet, heat oil over medium heat.*
Fry tortillas in hot oil for 5 to 10 seconds on each
side until lightly browned and blistered; drain
well on paper towels.

To serve, spread refried beans over each tortilla.
Spoon meat mixture over beans. Top with lettuce,
tomato, Guacamole and Salsa.

16 servings.

TIP: *For soft tortillas, omit frying in oil. Wrap
tortillas in foil; bake at 350° F. for about 5
minutes or until warm.

NUTRITION INFORMATION PER SERVING
SERVING SIZE: 1/16 OF RECIPE / PERCENT U.S. RDA PER SERVING

Calories	520	Protein	35%
Protein	22 g	Vitamin A	40%
Carbohydrate	41 g	Vitamin C	60%
Fat	30 g	Thiamine	20%
Cholesterol	53 mg	Riboflavin	20%
Sodium	1050 mg	Niacin	35%
Potassium	840 mg	Calcium	8%
		Iron	20%

Choffee Chiffon Cake

CAKE

7 eggs, separated
1 teaspoon cream of tartar
½ teaspoon salt
1 cup sugar
1 tablespoon instant coffee granules or crystals
⅓ cup water
1 cup all purpose or unbleached flour
2 ounces (2 squares) semi-sweet chocolate,
    grated
2 teaspoons vanilla

FROSTING

2 cups whipping cream
2 ounces (2 squares) semi-sweet chocolate,
    grated
⅓ cup powdered sugar
1½ teaspoons instant coffee granules or crystals
1 teaspoon vanilla

Heat oven to 325° F. In large bowl, beat egg
whites, cream of tartar and salt until mixture
forms soft peaks. Gradually add ½ cup of the
sugar, beating until *very stiff peaks* form. In small
bowl, beat egg yolks until very thick and lemon-
colored. Gradually add remaining ½ cup sugar,
beating until thick. Dissolve 1 tablespoon instant
coffee in water. Blend coffee mixture, flour, 2
ounces grated chocolate and 2 teaspoons vanilla
into egg yolk mixture. Beat 1 minute at low speed
or until just blended. Fold egg yolk mixture into
egg whites. Pour into ungreased 10-inch tube
pan. Bake at 325° F. for 50 to 60 minutes or until
cake springs back when touched lightly in center.
Invert cake on funnel or soft drink bottle; let
hang until completely cool. Remove cooled cake
from pan.

In large bowl, beat whipping cream until slightly
thickened. Reserve 1 tablespoon grated chocolate.
Add remaining grated chocolate, powdered sugar,
1½ teaspoons instant coffee and 1 teaspoon
vanilla to cream; beat until stiff peaks form (do
not overbeat). Slice cake into 2 layers. Fill cake
and frost sides and top; sprinkle reserved 1
tablespoon grated chocolate over top. Store in
refrigerator.

20 servings.

HIGH ALTITUDE—Above 3500 Feet: Increase
flour to 1 cup plus 3 tablespoons. Bake at 350° F.
for 45 to 55 minutes.

NUTRITION INFORMATION PER SERVING
SERVING SIZE: 1/20 OF RECIPE / PERCENT U.S. RDA PER SERVING

Calories	220	Protein	6%
Protein	4 g	Vitamin A	8%
Carbohydrate	22 g	Vitamin C	*
Fat	13 g	Thiamine	4%
Cholesterol	107 mg	Riboflavin	8%
Sodium	85 mg	Niacin	2%
Potassium	75 mg	Calcium	2%
		Iron	4%

*Contains less than 2% of the U.S. RDA of this nutrient.

Savory Stuffed Bread Snacks, page 28; Pea Pod Wrap-Ups, pages 28–29

Bridal Shower in Pastels

Serves 12
Orange Mint Slush*
Pea Pod Wrap-Ups*
Salmon Avocado Snacks*
Savory Stuffed Bread Snacks*
Shrimp Cocktail Tarts*
Meringue Fruit Medley*
Coffee   Tea
*Recipe included

"*H*ere comes the bride" (to be) to a lovingly planned, beautifully appointed shower of good wishes, exquisite foods and handsome presentation.

Our menu, an eye-pleasing selection of recipes in pastel tones of peach and green, is the epitome of elegance. Although foods are light and delicate in flavor and texture, they are appropriate for all seasons. In warmer weather, service on a porch or in the garden would be particularly lovely. In chilly weather, a roaring fire, fresh flower arrangements and cozy ambiance offer a welcoming atmosphere that is just as delightful.

Fresh fruits, crisp vegetables, delicate canapés and tantalizing tarts highlight the showy array. Although some preparation is required just before serving, much can be readied the day before or early on the party day. The slush keeps well in the freezer, while several recipes can be partially prepared early in the day and completed shortly before serving.

Looking for decorating ideas? Any florists' supply house is a good place to find tiny doves, lovebirds, ribbon, lace, silk flowers and other items to spark the imagination. It's always fun to tuck a tiny charm under a coffee cup to mark the next person to be married. And possibly provide a reason to plan another memorable bridal shower!

Preparation Timetable

Day Before Shower

Prepare *Orange Mint Slush;* cover and freeze • Refrigerate club soda • Prepare *Savory Stuffed Bread Snacks;* wrap and refrigerate • Clean and chop lettuce for *Shrimp Cocktail Tarts;* place in plastic bag and refrigerate.

Day of Shower

Early in the Day: Prepare meringue portion of *Meringue Fruit Medley;* cool completely • Prepare *Pea Pod Wrap-Ups;* cover and refrigerate • Bake tart shells for shrimp tarts; cool completely • Place shrimp in refrigerator to thaw.

Several Hours Before: Prepare filling and assemble meringue dessert; cover loosely and refrigerate.

Shortly Before Serving: About 30 minutes before serving, remove beverage from freezer and let stand at room temperature until slushy • Slice bread snacks and arrange on serving tray • Complete preparation of shrimp tarts • Prepare *Salmon Avocado Snacks* • Prepare coffee and/or tea • At serving time, add club soda to slush mixture for individual servings as stated in recipe.

Orange Mint Slush

2 cups sugar
7 cups water
¾ cup chopped fresh mint leaves
1 (12-ounce) can frozen orange juice concentrate, thawed
1 (6-ounce) can frozen lemonade concentrate, thawed
1 (1-liter) bottle (4¼ cups) club soda, chilled

In large saucepan, combine sugar, 3 cups of the water and mint leaves. Bring to a boil; reduce heat and simmer 2 minutes. Cool 1 hour. Strain and reserve liquid. In nonmetal container, combine reserved liquid, remaining 4 cups water and concentrates; cover and freeze.

To serve, let mixture stand at room temperature for 20 to 30 minutes or until slush consistency. Spoon about ½ cup slush mixture into each serving glass; pour ¼ cup of the club soda over each. Garnish with additional mint leaves, if desired.
15 (¾-cup) servings.

NUTRITION INFORMATION PER SERVING
SERVING SIZE: ¾ CUP

			PERCENT U.S. RDA PER SERVING
Calories	180	Protein	*
Protein	1 g	Vitamin A	*
Carbohydrate	44 g	Vitamin C	70%
Fat	0 g	Thiamine	6%
Cholesterol	0 mg	Riboflavin	*
Sodium	15 mg	Niacin	*
Potassium	200 mg	Calcium	*
		Iron	*

*Contains less than 2% of the U.S. RDA of this nutrient.

Salmon Avocado Snacks

1 ripe avocado
Lemon juice
3 ounces thinly sliced smoked salmon fillets, cut into 24 strips (½ × 2 × 2 inches)
Toothpicks
Fresh dill weed

Halve and peel avocado. Cut into 12 slices; cut each slice in half crosswise. Dip avocado pieces in lemon juice. Wrap a salmon slice around each avocado piece; secure with toothpick. Place sprig of fresh dill weed on top of each snack. Arrange on serving plate. Serve immediately.
24 snacks.

NUTRITION INFORMATION PER SERVING
SERVING SIZE: 1 SNACK

			PERCENT U.S. RDA PER SERVING
Calories	18	Protein	*
Protein	1 g	Vitamin A	2%
Carbohydrate	1 g	Vitamin C	2%
Fat	1 g	Thiamine	*
Cholesterol	1 mg	Riboflavin	*
Sodium	30 mg	Niacin	*
Potassium	60 mg	Calcium	*
		Iron	*

*Contains less than 2% of the U.S. RDA of this nutrient.

Savory Stuffed Bread Snacks

4 (6-inch) long sandwich rolls
1 (8-ounce) package cream cheese, softened
8 ounces (1⅓ cups) braunschweiger or liver sausage*
1 cup finely shredded carrots
½ cup chopped fresh parsley
2 tablespoons chopped green onions
2 teaspoons lemon juice
1 teaspoon Worcestershire sauce

Heat oven to 350° F. Cut about ½ inch off both ends of each roll; discard. Using teaspoon, remove bread from inside of roll, leaving about ¼ inch of crusty shell; set shells aside. Crumble soft bread pieces; place on cookie sheet. Toast bread crumbs at 350° F. for 12 to 15 minutes or until golden brown; cool.

In large bowl, combine cream cheese and braunschweiger; beat until smooth. By hand, stir in cooled bread crumbs and remaining ingredients. Spoon about 1 cup of filling mixture into each bread shell, pressing gently but firmly to remove air pockets. Wrap filled shells in plastic wrap or place in plastic bag. Refrigerate at least 4 hours or until serving time. To serve, unwrap, slice into ⅜-inch slices.
48 bread snacks.

TIPS: *Two 4½-ounce cans deviled ham can be substituted for braunschweiger.

To make ahead, prepare as directed above. Refrigerate up to 2 days before serving.

NUTRITION INFORMATION PER SERVING
SERVING SIZE: 1 BREAD SNACK

			PERCENT U.S. RDA PER SERVING
Calories	50	Protein	2%
Protein	2 g	Vitamin A	30%
Carbohydrate	4 g	Vitamin C	2%
Fat	3 g	Thiamine	2%
Cholesterol	13 mg	Riboflavin	6%
Sodium	105 mg	Niacin	2%
Potassium	35 mg	Calcium	*
		Iron	4%

*Contains less than 2% of the U.S. RDA of this nutrient.

Pea Pod Wrap-Ups

1 pound large fresh shrimp (about 35), cooked, shelled, deveined
1 (8-ounce) bottle prepared Dijon vinaigrette dressing
5 ounces fresh snow pea pods (about 35)
Toothpicks

Place shrimp in medium bowl. Pour dressing evenly over shrimp; stir to coat. Cover; refrigerate 1 hour. Meanwhile, remove strings from pea pods. To partially cook pea pods, place in boiling water for 1 minute or until pea pods turn bright green. Drain; rinse with cold water.

Drain dressing from shrimp. Wrap 1 pea pod around each shrimp; secure with toothpick. Cover; refrigerate until serving time.

About 35 appetizers.

NUTRITION INFORMATION PER SERVING
SERVING SIZE: 1   PERCENT U.S. RDA PER
APPETIZER   SERVING

Calories	18	Protein	2%
Protein	2 g	Vitamin A	*
Carbohydrate	0 g	Vitamin C	2%
Fat	1 g	Thiamine	*
Cholesterol	19 mg	Riboflavin	*
Sodium	35 mg	Niacin	*
Potassium	25 mg	Calcium	*
		Iron	2%

*Contains less than 2% of the U.S. RDA of this nutrient.

Shrimp Cocktail Tarts

1 (15-ounce) package refrigerated pie crusts
  Finely chopped leaf lettuce
1 (12-ounce) package frozen small cooked
    shrimp, thawed, rinsed, drained
  Cocktail sauce

Heat oven to 450° F. Allow both pie crust pouches to stand at room temperature for 15 to 20 minutes. Unfold each crust; remove top plastic sheet. Press out fold lines. Invert and remove remaining plastic sheet. Cut about ten 3-inch circles from each crust. Fit circles over backs of miniature muffin cups. Pinch 4 or 5 equally spaced pleats around sides of cup. Prick generously with fork. Bake at 450° F. for 9 to 13 minutes or until light golden brown. Cool completely; remove from muffin cups.

Place small amount of chopped lettuce in each tart shell. Spoon shrimp pieces over lettuce layer. Top with small amount of cocktail sauce. Garnish as desired.

20 appetizers.

NUTRITION INFORMATION PER SERVING
SERVING SIZE: 1   PERCENT U.S. RDA PER
APPETIZER   SERVING

Calories	120	Protein	6%
Protein	4 g	Vitamin A	2%
Carbohydrate	11 g	Vitamin C	2%
Fat	6 g	Thiamine	*
Cholesterol	39 mg	Riboflavin	*
Sodium	220 mg	Niacin	2%
Potassium	75 mg	Calcium	*
		Iron	2%

*Contains less than 2% of the U.S. RDA of this nutrient.

Meringue Fruit Medley

MERINGUE
 4 egg whites
¼ teaspoon cream of tartar
⅔ cup sugar

FILLING
 1 cup sugar
 2 teaspoons grated lemon peel
½ cup margarine or butter
⅓ cup lemon juice
 4 egg yolks
 1 cup whipping cream, whipped

TOPPING
 Select from the following fruit choices:
   Thinly sliced honeydew melon pieces, rind
     removed
   Thinly sliced cantaloupe pieces, rind
     removed
   Seedless green grapes
   Sliced nectarines
   Mandarin orange segments, drained
   Kiwifruit, peeled, sliced, slices halved

Heat oven to 275° F. Line cookie sheet with brown paper or parchment paper. In large bowl, beat egg whites and cream of tartar until soft peaks form. Add ⅔ cup sugar 1 tablespoon at a time, beating continuously until soft peaks form and mixture is glossy, about 1½ minutes. Spread meringue onto paper-lined cookie sheet in 12 × 5-inch rectangle. Using back of spoon, form a 1-inch-high edge around all sides. Bake at 275° F. for 60 to 75 minutes or until light golden brown and dry. Cool completely.

In heavy 2-quart saucepan, combine 1 cup sugar, lemon peel, margarine and lemon juice; heat until margarine is melted, stirring occasionally. Using wire whisk, blend in egg yolks. Cook over medium heat, whisking constantly, until mixture comes to a full boil, about 5 minutes. Boil 2 minutes, whisking constantly. Cool 15 minutes. Cover top surface with waxed paper; refrigerate until thoroughly chilled. Fold whipped cream into cooled lemon mixture. Spoon evenly into meringue shell. Arrange fruit in rows alternating orange- and green-colored fruit. Refrigerate until serving time.

12 servings.

NUTRITION INFORMATION PER SERVING
SERVING SIZE: 1/12 OF   PERCENT U.S. RDA PER
RECIPE   SERVING

Calories	290	Protein	4%
Protein	3 g	Vitamin A	20%
Carbohydrate	32 g	Vitamin C	25%
Fat	17 g	Thiamine	*
Cholesterol	100 mg	Riboflavin	6%
Sodium	120 mg	Niacin	*
Potassium	125 mg	Calcium	2%
		Iron	*

*Contains less than 2% of the U.S. RDA of this nutrient.

Hearts and Flowers Reception Cake, page 33

Hearts and Flowers Wedding Reception

Serves 25
Rosy Reception Punch*
Cashew Pasta Chicken Salad*
Petits Croissants
Frosted Heart Cookies* Candy-Covered Berries*
Hearts and Flowers Reception Cake*
Coffee Tea
*Recipe included

*I*f you are fortunate enough to be hosting a wedding reception, we think you will find this elegant menu as enchanting as it is economical and easy to prepare. It is, of course, time for a dazzling display of your best linens and tableware because this splendid event must be a feast for the eyes as well as the palate.

If you are involved in the wedding in any way, consider arranging for kitchen and serving help. Even with buffet service, you want to be free of food-related duties to greet guests and circulate during the reception. Invite special friends of the bridal couple (who are not members of the wedding party) to assist with pouring punch, coffee and tea. This adds a gracious personal touch and allows the honored helpers to visit while assigned to a special post. For additional information about serving large groups, see Entertaining with Enthusiasm.

Our selection of foods is light and well suited to a flexible serving time from early afternoon through the supper hour. The Hearts and Flowers Reception Cake is truly magnificent. No special baking pans are required and a cake mix minimizes preparation time and effort. It can be prepared months ahead and frozen. Decorating, however, should be done the day of the reception. For fifty people, you will need two cakes. An option is to decorate one cake entirely and have the other frosted only and cut into serving squares on a dessert table.

Preparation Timetable

Several Days Ahead
Bake cakes for *Hearts and Flowers Reception Cake* but do not frost; cool completely, wrap and freeze.

Day Before Reception
Place grapefruit juice concentrate in refrigerator to thaw and refrigerate carbonated beverage for *Rosy Reception Punch;* prepare decorative ice ring and freeze • Cook and cube chicken for *Cashew Pasta Chicken Salad;* cover and refrigerate • Prepare *Frosted Heart Cookies;* after frosting has dried, place in covered container and store at room temperature •

Day of Reception
Early in the Day: Remove cakes from freezer to thaw; one to two hours later, assemble, frost and decorate cake • Cook macaroni and combine all ingredients for chicken salad except cashews and lettuce; cover and refrigerate • Prepare *Candy-Covered Berries;* cover loosely and refrigerate • Prepare juice mixture for punch; refrigerate.

Several Hours Before: Arrange cookies and berries on serving trays; cover.

Shortly Before Serving: Add cashews to chicken salad; spoon into lettuce-lined serving bowl • Prepare coffee and/or tea • Complete preparation of punch; garnish bowl with ice ring • Place croissants in bread basket.

Rosy Reception Punch

9½ cups water
 1 (12-ounce) can frozen grapefruit juice concentrate, thawed
 1 (5.5-ounce) package raspberry-flavored sugar-sweetened soft drink mix
 1 (2-liter) bottle (8½ cups) lemon-lime-flavored carbonated beverage, chilled
   Ice or ice ring

In 6-quart nonmetal container, combine water, juice concentrate and soft drink mix; blend well. Refrigerate until thoroughly chilled. Just before serving, combine juice mixture and carbonated beverage in a large punch bowl. Serve over ice or float ice ring in punch bowl. Garnish as desired. **40 (½-cup) servings.**

NUTRITION INFORMATION PER SERVING
SERVING SIZE: ½ CUP

		PERCENT U.S. RDA PER SERVING
Calories	50	Protein	*
Protein	0 g	Vitamin A	*
Carbohydrate	13 g	Vitamin C	30%
Fat	0 g	Thiamine	*
Cholesterol	0 mg	Riboflavin	*
Sodium	10 mg	Niacin	*
Potassium	50 mg	Calcium	*
		Iron	*

*Contains less than 2% of the U.S. RDA of this nutrient.

Cashew Pasta Chicken Salad

 16 ounces (7 cups) uncooked bow tie or large shell macaroni
  9 cups cubed cooked chicken*
  2 cups sliced celery
  ½ cup sliced green onions
  ¼ cup chopped pimiento, drained
  1 teaspoon salt
  1 (16-ounce) package frozen sweet peas, thawed, drained
  2 (4.5-ounce) jars sliced mushrooms, drained
  2 cups prepared buttermilk-flavored ranch dressing**
  1 to 1½ cups whole cashews
    Lettuce leaves

Cook macaroni to desired doneness as directed on package. Drain; rinse with cold water. Place cooked macaroni in 7-quart bowl or plastic container. Add remaining ingredients except cashews and lettuce; toss gently. Refrigerate until serving time. Add cashews; toss gently. Serve in lettuce-lined bowl.
25 (1-cup) servings.

TIPS: *A 3-pound frying chicken, cooked, skinned and boned, will yield about 3 cups cubed chicken.

**One 1-ounce package buttermilk-flavored ranch dressing, prepared according to package directions, makes 2 cups prepared dressing.

NUTRITION INFORMATION PER SERVING
SERVING SIZE: 1 CUP

		PERCENT U.S. RDA PER SERVING
Calories	290	Protein	30%
Protein	20 g	Vitamin A	2%
Carbohydrate	20 g	Vitamin C	8%
Fat	15 g	Thiamine	20%
Cholesterol	45 mg	Riboflavin	10%
Sodium	340 mg	Niacin	35%
Potassium	290 mg	Calcium	2%
		Iron	10%

Frosted Heart Cookies

COOKIES
 1 (20-ounce) package refrigerated sliceable sugar cookie dough, well chilled
 ⅓ cup powdered sugar
 1 tablespoon flour

FROSTING
 2 cups powdered sugar
 ⅛ teaspoon salt
 ¼ cup margarine or butter, softened
 ¼ cup shortening
 2 to 4 tablespoons milk
 ½ teaspoon vanilla
   Food color

Heat oven to 350° F. For easier handling, work with half of dough at a time; refrigerate remainder of roll until needed. Combine ⅓ cup powdered sugar and flour; sprinkle half of mixture on work surface. Coat sides of half roll of well-chilled dough with sugar mixture. Roll out to about ⅛-inch thickness. Cut with 2-inch heart-shaped cookie cutter dipped in sugar mixture. Place cookies 2 inches apart on ungreased cookie sheets. Bake at 350° F. for 7 to 9 minutes or until light golden brown. Cool 1 minute; remove from cookie sheets. Cool completely. Repeat with remaining dough.

In medium bowl, combine all frosting ingredients except food color; beat until smooth and of desired spreading consistency. Add desired amount of food color. Pipe or spread on cooled cookies; allow frosting to dry. Store cookies in single layer in covered container.
4 dozen cookies.

NUTRITION INFORMATION PER SERVING
SERVING SIZE: 1 COOKIE

		PERCENT U.S. RDA PER SERVING
Calories	90	Protein	*
Protein	1 g	Vitamin A	*
Carbohydrate	12 g	Vitamin C	*
Fat	4 g	Thiamine	2%
Cholesterol	0 mg	Riboflavin	2%
Sodium	70 mg	Niacin	*
Potassium	10 mg	Calcium	*
		Iron	*

*Contains less than 2% of the U.S. RDA of this nutrient.

Hearts and Flowers Reception Cake

CAKE
2 packages pudding-included white cake mix
2½ cups water
4 tablespoons oil
2 eggs

FROSTING
¾ cup shortening
¾ cup margarine or butter
¼ teaspoon salt
1 teaspoon vanilla
6 cups powdered sugar
2 tablespoons lemon juice
2 to 3 tablespoons milk
4 teaspoons grated lemon peel

Decorating bag and tips

Heat oven to 325° F. Grease and flour one 9-inch square pan and one 9-inch round cake pan. Line each pan with waxed paper and grease again. In large bowl, combine 1 package of the cake mix, 1¼ cups of the water, 2 tablespoons of the oil and 1 of the eggs at low speed until moistened; beat 2 minutes at high speed. Pour half of the batter into each greased, floured and lined pan. Bake at 325° F. for 25 to 35 minutes or until toothpick inserted in center comes out clean. Cool 15 minutes; carefully remove cake from pans. Remove waxed paper and cool cakes completely. Repeat with second cake mix and remaining water, oil and egg. Trim 1½ inches evenly from sides of 1 cooled square cake and 1 cooled round cake. (Store cake trimmings in covered container for a later use as desired.)

In large bowl, beat shortening and margarine until light and fluffy. Add salt and vanilla. Beat in powdered sugar 1 cup at a time, frequently scraping bottom and sides of bowl. Beat in lemon juice and enough milk for desired spreading consistency. Reserve 2 cups frosting for piping. Add lemon peel to remaining frosting; beat at high speed until light and fluffy.

To assemble cake, cover 18 × 14-inch rectangle or heart-shaped heavy cardboard with foil or colored paper. Cut each 9-inch round cake in half to form 2 semicircles. Following diagram, arrange untrimmed square cake and 2 untrimmed round cake halves on foil-covered cardboard to form heart. Spread top evenly with ½ cup of frosting. Arrange trimmed square cake and 2 trimmed round cake halves over first layer, making sure second layer is centered evenly over first layer.

Frost sides and top of cake. Using reserved frosting, decorating bag and writing tip, pipe small dots randomly on sides and top of cake. Using shell or star tip, pipe rope design around edge of layers. Garnish as desired.
25 servings.

HIGH ALTITUDE—Above 3500 Feet: Add 2 tablespoons flour to each package of dry cake mix. Bake as directed above.

NUTRITION INFORMATION PER SERVING

SERVING SIZE: 1/25 OF RECIPE		PERCENT U.S. RDA PER SERVING	
Calories	400	Protein	4%
Protein	2 g	Vitamin A	4%
Carbohydrate	57 g	Vitamin C	*
Fat	18 g	Thiamine	6%
Cholesterol	17 mg	Riboflavin	4%
Sodium	340 mg	Niacin	4%
Potassium	30 mg	Calcium	6%
		Iron	2%

*Contains less than 2% of the U.S. RDA of this nutrient.

Candy-Covered Berries

36 large strawberries

DARK CHOCOLATE COATING
½ cup semi-sweet chocolate chips
1 teaspoon oil

WHITE CHOCOLATE COATING
½ cup vanilla milk chips
1½ teaspoons oil

Wash strawberries; gently pat dry. Line tray with waxed paper. In small saucepan over low heat, melt chocolate chips and 1 teaspoon oil, stirring occasionally until smooth. Remove from heat. Set saucepan in pan of hot water to maintain dipping consistency. Dip 18 strawberries into chocolate mixture until ⅔ of each strawberry is coated. Allow excess chocolate to drip off; place strawberries stem side down on paper-lined tray. Refrigerate until serving time. Repeat with remaining strawberries, using vanilla milk chips and 1½ teaspoons oil.
36 berries.

TIP: To make pastel-colored coating, add 3 to 5 drops any food color to melted vanilla milk chip mixture.

NUTRITION INFORMATION PER SERVING

SERVING SIZE: 1 STRAWBERRY		PERCENT U.S. RDA PER SERVING	
Calories	35	Protein	*
Protein	0 g	Vitamin A	*
Carbohydrate	4 g	Vitamin C	15%
Fat	2 g	Thiamine	*
Cholesterol	0 mg	Riboflavin	*
Sodium	0 mg	Niacin	*
Potassium	45 mg	Calcium	*
		Iron	*

*Contains less than 2% of the U.S. RDA of this nutrient.

Pictured clockwise from top left: Picadillo Dip with tortilla chips, page 37; Marinated Olives, page 36; Empanadas, page 37

Housewarming Tapas Buffet

Serves 20
White Wine Sangria*
and/or
Tangy Apple-Orange Refresher*
Marinated Cucumbers*   *Marinated Olives**
Celery Boats*   *Picadillo Dip**   *Tortilla Chips*
Green and White Bean Salad*   *Assorted Bakery Breads*
Empanadas*
Chicken and Mushrooms in Sherry Sauce*
Shrimp on Rye Canapés*
Summer Peach Mousse*   *Chocolate Shortbread**
Coffee   Tea
*Recipe included

Americans aren't alone in their love of snacking. These Spanish hors d'oeuvres, or tapas, originated years ago when bartenders placed plain bread rounds over glasses of sweet wines to discourage insects. Eventually, these "lids" were topped with savory bits of meat, fish, cheeses, olives and other Mediterranean staples. A culinary custom was born.

Another popular Spanish and South American culinary delight, empanadas, are tasty turnovers with a savory or sweet filling, depending on the whim of the chef. Refrigerated pie crust makes preparation a breeze and because the filling is neatly contained, the little meat pies are perfect finger food for an appetizer buffet such as this.

Variety definitely is the focal point of this splendid sampler and there is ample food for at least twenty guests. To avoid last-minute confusion, have your buffet table arranged well in advance. Vary colors, textures and heights using an eye-catching mixture of serving dishes—footed bowls, pedestal servers and flat platters. We suggest two serving lines, one on each side of the table, with easy access to small plates, napkins and appetizer or salad forks.

Each recipe has been streamlined so final touches are minimal. For best results and ease in handling, prepare the Summer Peach Mousse twice rather than doubling the recipe. Although sangria usually is poured from a glass pitcher, it can be served from a punch bowl.

Preparation Timetable

Several Days Ahead

Refrigerate wine and soda for *White Wine Sangria* and/or carbonated beverage for *Tangy Apple-Orange Refresher* • Prepare *Marinated Olives* and *Green and White Bean Salad;* cover and refrigerate • Prepare *Empanadas;* wrap airtight and freeze • Prepare *Chocolate Shortbread;* cover and store at room temperature.

Day Before Buffet

Prepare fruit in sugar syrup for sangria; cover and refrigerate • Prepare *Marinated Cucumbers* and *Picadillo Dip;* cover each and refrigerate • Prepare *Summer Peach Mousse* twice; cover and refrigerate.

Day of Buffet

<u>Early in the Day:</u> Remove empanadas from freezer to thaw.

<u>Several Hours Before:</u> Combine fruit juices and lemonade concentrate for refresher beverage; cover and freeze • Prepare *Celery Boats, Shrimp on Rye Canapés* and *Chicken and Mushrooms in Sherry Sauce;* cover each and refrigerate.

<u>Shortly Before Serving:</u> Reheat dip, chicken and empanadas • Prepare coffee and/or tea • Complete preparation of beverage(s).

White Wine Sangria

1 cup sugar
1 cup water
1 cinnamon stick
2 medium oranges, sliced
1 lemon, sliced
1 lime, sliced
3 (750-milliliter) bottles dry white wine, chilled
3 cups club soda, chilled

In medium saucepan, combine sugar and water; add cinnamon stick. Simmer over low heat 5 minutes. Remove from heat; add fruit to sugar syrup. Cool completely; remove cinnamon stick.

In large nonmetal pitcher, combine ½ cup of syrup, 1 cup of fruit, 1 bottle of wine and 1 cup of club soda. As needed, repeat with remaining ingredients.
24 (½-cup) servings.

NUTRITION INFORMATION PER SERVING
SERVING SIZE: ½ CUP

		PERCENT U.S. RDA PER SERVING	
Calories	100	Protein	*
Protein	0 g	Vitamin A	*
Carbohydrate	11 g	Vitamin C	10%
Fat	0 g	Thiamine	*
Cholesterol	0 mg	Riboflavin	*
Sodium	10 mg	Niacin	*
Potassium	105 mg	Calcium	*
		Iron	*

*Contains less than 2% of the U.S. RDA of this nutrient.

Marinated Olives

1 (16-ounce) can pitted ripe olives, drained
1 (16-ounce) jar pimiento-stuffed olives, drained
½ cup chopped onion
1 teaspoon dried thyme leaves
2 tablespoons red wine vinegar
2 garlic cloves, finely chopped
1 lemon, sliced
1½ to 2 cups water

In 1-quart nonmetal container, combine all ingredients except water. Add enough water to cover olives. Cover; refrigerate 2 to 3 days. To serve, remove olives with slotted spoon.
4 cups; about 20 servings.

NUTRITION INFORMATION: Variables in this recipe make it impossible to calculate nutrition information.

Tangy Apple-Orange Refresher

1 quart (4 cups) apple juice
1 quart (4 cups) orange juice
1 (6-ounce) can frozen lemonade concentrate, thawed
1 (1-liter) bottle (4¼ cups) lemon-lime carbonated beverage, chilled

In 4-quart nonmetal container, combine juices and lemonade concentrate; stir until well blended.* Cover; freeze 2½ to 3 hours or until slushy. Spoon slush mixture into punch bowl; stir in carbonated beverage. Garnish as desired.
25 (½-cup) servings.

TIP: *A clean 5-quart ice cream bucket can be used as a container.

NUTRITION INFORMATION PER SERVING
SERVING SIZE: ½ CUP

		PERCENT U.S. RDA PER SERVING	
Calories	70	Protein	*
Protein	0 g	Vitamin A	*
Carbohydrate	17 g	Vitamin C	30%
Fat	0 g	Thiamine	2%
Cholesterol	0 mg	Riboflavin	*
Sodium	10 mg	Niacin	*
Potassium	130 mg	Calcium	*
		Iron	*

*Contains less than 2% of the U.S. RDA of this nutrient.

Marinated Cucumbers

6 cups (4 medium) thinly sliced cucumbers
½ cup chopped onion
2 medium red or green bell peppers, cut into thin strips
2 cups sugar
2 teaspoons salt
1 teaspoon celery seed
1 teaspoon mustard seed
1 cup cider vinegar

In large nonmetal bowl, combine cucumbers, onion and red peppers. In medium bowl, combine remaining ingredients; blend well. Pour over cucumber mixture; toss to coat. Cover; refrigerate at least 24 hours, stirring occasionally. If desired, drain before serving.
24 (¼-cup) servings.

NUTRITION INFORMATION PER SERVING
SERVING SIZE: ¼ CUP

		PERCENT U.S. RDA PER SERVING	
Calories	80	Protein	*
Protein	0 g	Vitamin A	6%
Carbohydrate	19 g	Vitamin C	20%
Fat	0 g	Thiamine	*
Cholesterol	0 mg	Riboflavin	*
Sodium	180 mg	Niacin	*
Potassium	70 mg	Calcium	*
		Iron	*

*Contains less than 2% of the U.S. RDA of this nutrient.

Celery Boats

1 (6.5-ounce) can tuna, drained, flaked
¼ cup chopped pimiento-stuffed olives
2 tablespoons chopped onion
1 tablespoon capers, drained
2 tablespoons mayonnaise
20 (2½-inch) pieces celery

In small bowl, combine all ingredients except celery; mix well. Fill celery pieces with tuna mixture. Cover; refrigerate until serving time. **20 servings.**

NUTRITION INFORMATION PER SERVING

SERVING SIZE: 1/20 OF RECIPE		PERCENT U.S. RDA PER SERVING	
Calories	25	Protein	4%
Protein	3 g	Vitamin A	*
Carbohydrate	1 g	Vitamin C	4%
Fat	1 g	Thiamine	*
Cholesterol	2 mg	Riboflavin	*
Sodium	45 mg	Niacin	4%
Potassium	65 mg	Calcium	*
		Iron	*

*Contains less than 2% of the U.S. RDA of this nutrient.

Empanadas

2 (15-ounce) packages refrigerated pie crusts

FILLING
½ pound ground beef
½ cup chopped onion
2 garlic cloves, minced
½ teaspoon dried oregano leaves
½ teaspoon cumin
¼ teaspoon sugar
½ cup dry red wine
2 tablespoons whipping cream or milk
4 eggs, hard-cooked, chopped*

Allow crust pouches to stand at room temperature for 15 to 20 minutes. Meanwhile, in medium skillet brown ground beef, onion and garlic; drain. Stir in oregano, cumin, sugar and wine; simmer 5 minutes or until wine has evaporated. Remove from heat; stir in whipping cream. Cool.

Heat oven to 400° F. Unfold each pie crust; remove top plastic sheet. Press out fold lines. Invert and remove remaining plastic sheet. Cut five 4-inch circles from each crust. Place about 1 tablespoon meat mixture on each circle; top with chopped egg. Brush edges of dough with water. Fold circle in half over filling; press edges with fork to seal. Place on ungreased cookie sheets. Bake at 400° F. for 15 to 20 minutes or until light golden brown. Serve warm, or cool on wire rack and reheat before serving. **20 turnovers.**

TIP: *To hard-cook eggs, place in saucepan; cover with cold water. Bring to a boil; reduce heat and simmer very gently for 15 minutes. Cool eggs under cold running water to stop cooking. Refrigerate.

NUTRITION INFORMATION PER SERVING

SERVING SIZE: 1 TURNOVER		PERCENT U.S. RDA PER SERVING	
Calories	240	Protein	6%
Protein	5 g	Vitamin A	2%
Carbohydrate	20 g	Vitamin C	*
Fat	15 g	Thiamine	*
Cholesterol	62 mg	Riboflavin	4%
Sodium	190 mg	Niacin	2%
Potassium	75 mg	Calcium	*
		Iron	2%

*Contains less than 2% of the U.S. RDA of this nutrient.

Picadillo Dip

1 pound ground beef
1 cup water
½ teaspoon salt
¼ teaspoon pepper
1 garlic clove, minced
½ cup raisins
½ cup slivered almonds
¼ cup chopped pimiento-stuffed olives
1 tablespoon capers, drained
½ teaspoon sugar
1 (16-ounce) can (2 cups) tomatoes, undrained, cut up
1 (6-ounce) can tomato paste
   Round tortilla chips

In medium saucepan over medium heat, brown ground beef. Add water, salt, pepper and garlic; simmer 20 minutes. Drain. Add remaining ingredients except tortilla chips; mix well. Cook over low heat about 45 minutes or until thickened, stirring occasionally. Serve hot with tortilla chips. **4 cups.**

MICROWAVE DIRECTIONS: In 2-quart microwave-safe casserole or bowl, microwave ground beef on HIGH for 5 to 6 minutes or until no longer pink, stirring twice. Add water, salt, pepper and garlic. Microwave on HIGH for 5 to 6 minutes or until mixture comes to a boil. Drain. Add remaining ingredients except tortilla chips; mix well. Microwave on HIGH for 6 to 8 minutes or until very hot, stirring once halfway through cooking. Serve hot with tortilla chips.

NUTRITION INFORMATION PER SERVING

SERVING SIZE: 1 TABLESPOON DIP		PERCENT U.S. RDA PER SERVING	
Calories	35	Protein	2%
Protein	2 g	Vitamin A	2%
Carbohydrate	2 g	Vitamin C	4%
Fat	2 g	Thiamine	*
Cholesterol	4 mg	Riboflavin	*
Sodium	65 mg	Niacin	2%
Potassium	70 mg	Calcium	*
		Iron	*

*Contains less than 2% of the U.S. RDA of this nutrient.

Green and White Bean Salad

Green and White Bean Salad

DRESSING
⅔ cup lemon juice
⅔ cup olive oil or vegetable oil
1 teaspoon salt
1 teaspoon sugar
½ teaspoon pepper
1 teaspoon anchovy paste, if desired
2 garlic cloves, finely minced

SALAD
3 (15.5-ounce) cans Great Northern beans, drained
3 cups frozen cut green beans, cooked, drained
3 medium tomatoes, chopped
¾ cup thinly sliced red onion

In medium bowl or jar with tight-fitting lid, combine all dressing ingredients; shake well. In large bowl, combine all salad ingredients. Pour dressing over salad; toss gently. Cover; refrigerate at least 4 hours to blend flavors.
20 (½-cup) servings.

TIP: The flavors of this salad improve with time. It can be prepared, covered and refrigerated for up to 3 days before serving.

NUTRITION INFORMATION PER SERVING
SERVING SIZE: ½ CUP

		PERCENT U.S. RDA PER SERVING	
Calories	140	Protein	4%
Protein	4 g	Vitamin A	4%
Carbohydrate	12 g	Vitamin C	10%
Fat	8 g	Thiamine	2%
Cholesterol	0 mg	Riboflavin	2%
Sodium	210 mg	Niacin	*
Potassium	130 mg	Calcium	6%
		Iron	6%

*Contains less than 2% of the U.S. RDA of this nutrient.

Chicken and Mushrooms in Sherry Sauce

⅓ cup oil
6 whole chicken breasts, skinned, boned, cut into ½-inch cubes
½ cup chopped onion
2 garlic cloves, minced
¼ cup flour
1 teaspoon salt
1 teaspoon lemon pepper seasoning
1 cup dry sherry
1 cup chicken broth
2 teaspoons lemon juice
2 bay leaves
4 (4.5-ounce) jars whole mushrooms, drained

In large skillet, heat oil over medium-high heat. Add chicken; stir until chicken is thoroughly cooked. Remove chicken with slotted spoon. Add onion and garlic; cook until tender. Stir in flour, salt and lemon pepper seasoning; mix well. Gradually add sherry, chicken broth, lemon juice and bay leaves. Cook over medium heat about 3 minutes or until thickened. Add chicken and mushrooms; simmer 5 minutes or until thoroughly heated. Remove bay leaves.
24 (½-cup) servings.

NUTRITION INFORMATION PER SERVING
SERVING SIZE: ½ CUP

		PERCENT U.S. RDA PER SERVING	
Calories	120	Protein	20%
Protein	14 g	Vitamin A	*
Carbohydrate	3 g	Vitamin C	*
Fat	5 g	Thiamine	2%
Cholesterol	37 mg	Riboflavin	2%
Sodium	230 mg	Niacin	30%
Potassium	150 mg	Calcium	*
		Iron	2%

*Contains less than 2% of the U.S. RDA of this nutrient.

Shrimp on Rye Canapés

2 (4½-ounce) cans broken shrimp, drained,
   rinsed, finely chopped
½ cup mayonnaise or salad dressing
⅓ cup finely chopped onion
¼ cup finely chopped celery
1 tablespoon chopped fresh parsley
2 teaspoons lemon juice
¼ teaspoon salt
1 (16-ounce) loaf sliced snack rye bread
   Fresh dill weed or dried dill weed, if desired

In small bowl, combine shrimp, mayonnaise, onion, celery, parsley, lemon juice and salt; mix well. Spread on rye bread slices. Garnish with fresh dill weed. Cover; refrigerate until serving time.
About 40 appetizers.

NUTRITION INFORMATION PER SERVING
SERVING SIZE: 1   PERCENT U.S. RDA PER
APPETIZER   SERVING

Calories	60	Protein	4%
Protein	3 g	Vitamin A	*
Carbohydrate	6 g	Vitamin C	2%
Fat	2 g	Thiamine	2%
Cholesterol	13 mg	Riboflavin	*
Sodium	105 mg	Niacin	2%
Potassium	40 mg	Calcium	*
		Iron	2%

*Contains less than 2% of the U.S. RDA of this nutrient.

Chocolate Shortbread

1 cup powdered sugar
1 cup unsalted butter, softened
1 teaspoon vanilla
2 cups all purpose or unbleached flour
¼ cup unsweetened cocoa

Heat oven to 325° F. In large bowl, beat powdered sugar and butter until light and fluffy. Add vanilla; blend well. Lightly spoon flour into measuring cup; level off. Stir in flour and cocoa; mix well. On ungreased cookie sheet, press dough out to form 12 × 6-inch rectangle about ½ inch thick. Prick thoroughly with fork. Bake at 325° F. for 20 minutes or until dough is slightly firm to touch. Immediately cut into desired shape.* Cool 5 minutes; remove from cookie sheet. Cool completely on wire rack.
32 cookies.

TIP: *To make triangle shape, cut dough crosswise into four 3-inch strips. Cut strips in half lengthwise forming eight 3 × 3-inch squares. Divide each square into 4 triangles by cutting diagonally from corner to corner.

HIGH ALTITUDE—Above 3500 Feet: No change.

NUTRITION INFORMATION PER SERVING
SERVING SIZE: 1   PERCENT U.S. RDA PER
COOKIE   SERVING

Calories	90	Protein	*
Protein	1 g	Vitamin A	4%
Carbohydrate	9 g	Vitamin C	*
Fat	6 g	Thiamine	4%
Cholesterol	16 mg	Riboflavin	2%
Sodium	5 mg	Niacin	2%
Potassium	15 mg	Calcium	*
		Iron	2%

*Contains less than 2% of the U.S. RDA of this nutrient.

Summer Peach Mousse

1 (3-ounce) package peach-flavored gelatin
1 cup boiling water
2 cups sliced, peeled ripe peaches*
2 tablespoons honey
¼ teaspoon almond extract
1 cup whipping cream, whipped
   Fresh peach slices
   Fresh blueberries or raspberries

In large bowl, dissolve gelatin in boiling water. In blender container or food processor bowl with metal blade, combine peaches, honey and almond extract; blend until smooth. Stir peach mixture into gelatin. Cover; refrigerate until thickened but not set, 1 to 1½ hours. Beat gelatin mixture at highest speed until doubled in volume, about 5 minutes. Fold in whipped cream. Pour into 1½-quart bowl. Cover; refrigerate until firm, about 4 hours. Serve mousse with peach slices and berries.
10 (½-cup) servings.

TIP: *Two cups canned sliced peaches, drained, or one 16-ounce package frozen peach slices without syrup, thawed, can be substituted for fresh peaches.

NUTRITION INFORMATION PER SERVING
SERVING SIZE: ½ CUP   PERCENT U.S. RDA PER
                                          SERVING

Calories	160	Protein	2%
Protein	2 g	Vitamin A	10%
Carbohydrate	17 g	Vitamin C	6%
Fat	9 g	Thiamine	*
Cholesterol	33 mg	Riboflavin	2%
Sodium	35 mg	Niacin	2%
Potassium	125 mg	Calcium	*
		Iron	*

*Contains less than 2% of the U.S. RDA of this nutrient.

Pictured clockwise from upper left: Pear-Walnut Salad, page 42; Stuffed Fillet of Sole in Puff Pastry, page 42; Orange Marjoram Carrots, page 43

Wedding Anniversary Seafood Dinner

Serves 4

Chilled Champagne or White Wine
Pear-Walnut Salad*
Stuffed Fillet of Sole in Puff Pastry*
Orange Marjoram Carrots*
Apricot-Yogurt Cheesecake*
Special Friends Cappuccino*

*Recipe included

---

*T*his romantic repast gives new meaning to the word "special." Host this elegant dinner for four for your favorite anniversary couple, or for your own anniversary, invite a set of parents or a couple from the wedding party or two other close friends who would appreciate sharing in the celebration. Or, since each recipe doubles easily, expand the party to eight.

Although preparation time is a bit longer than for many of the menus in this collection, the results are spectacular enough to warrant the extra attention and the elegant touches. And some make-ahead steps and the use of convenience products like frozen puff pastry help streamline the work considerably. The main attraction, a delicate fillet of sole, is beautifully housed in a flaky casing and embellished with colorful carrots. Incidentally, the entire menu is a terrific testimonial for the artful use of herbs as a way to reduce the need for salt as a flavor enhancer. Thyme, bay leaves, celery seed, parsley and marjoram—all are featured with fantastic results.

Apricot-Yogurt Cheesecake is a no-bake beauty you will want to serve as dessert on this and many other occasions. Warm and satisfying liqueur-laced cappuccino completes this elegant meal. The mix for this makes a wonderful hostess gift—perfect for a holiday gift. Place in an appropriately decorated container and attach mixing and storage instructions.

Preparation Timetable

Day Before

• Refrigerate champagne or wine • Prepare mix for *Special Friends Cappuccino;* cover and refrigerate • Prepare dressing and toast walnuts for *Pear-Walnut Salad.* Cover and refrigerate dressing; store walnuts at room temperature • Prepare *Apricot-Yogurt Cheesecake;* cover and refrigerate.

Day of Dinner

Early in the Day: Prepare filling for *Stuffed Fillet of Sole in Puff Pastry;* cover and refrigerate • Wash lettuce for salad; refrigerate.

One Hour Before: Assemble fish and pastry; refrigerate • Remove springform pan from cheesecake; place cheesecake on serving plate and refrigerate • Prepare topping for cheesecake; place in serving bowl.

Shortly Before Serving: Slice pears for salad; arrange salads on plates or toss all salad ingredients in large bowl • Prepare *Orange Marjoram Carrots;* keep warm • Complete preparation of fish entree; keep warm • Just before serving dessert, prepare topping for cheesecake • Prepare and serve cappuccino after dessert.

Stuffed Fillet of Sole in Puff Pastry

FILLING
1 tablespoon butter or margarine
½ cup zucchini, cut into julienne strips
    1 × ¼ × ¼ inches long
¼ cup red bell pepper, cut into julienne strips
    1 × ¼ × ¼ inches long
1 tablespoon chopped shallots
½ pound medium-sized uncooked shrimp,
    shelled, deveined, cut into ½-inch pieces
Salt and pepper
4 sole fillets, cut in half crosswise*

PUFF PASTRY
1 sheet frozen puff pastry
1 egg
1 tablespoon water

BUTTER SAUCE
2 tablespoons chopped shallots
½ cup white wine
¼ cup white wine vinegar
12 tablespoons butter, room temperature
1 tablespoon chopped fresh parsley
½ teaspoon grated lemon peel

In small skillet, melt 1 tablespoon butter; add zucchini, red pepper, 1 tablespoon shallots and shrimp. Cook over medium-high heat for 1 to 2 minutes or until vegetables are crisp-tender and shrimp turn pink. Salt and pepper to taste; cool.

Remove puff pastry from freezer; allow to stand at room temperature for 20 minutes. Lightly grease cookie sheet. Heat oven to 400° F. Open pastry sheet; cut into squares. Roll out each quarter into a 7-inch square; place on greased cookie sheet. Pat each fish fillet dry. Place 1 fish fillet half in center of each pastry square. Using a slotted spoon, spoon about ¼ cup of filling onto each piece of fish. Top with remaining fillet halves. In small bowl, beat egg and 1 tablespoon water. Brush edges of each pastry with egg mixture. Bring 4 corners of each pastry square to center; pinch center and edges firmly to seal. Brush tops of pastry with egg mixture. Prick each with fork to vent steam.** Bake at 400° F. for 18 to 22 minutes or until deep golden brown.

In small saucepan, combine 2 tablespoons shallots, wine and vinegar; bring to a boil. Boil mixture until reduced to ½ cup. Over low heat using whisk, beat in 12 tablespoons butter, 1 tablespoon at a time. Do not add more butter until preceding tablespoon is completely beaten in.*** Add parsley and lemon peel. Keep warm over hot water. Serve warm sauce with pastry-wrapped fish.
4 servings.

TIPS: *If using frozen fish fillets, thaw completely.

**Pastry-wrapped fish can be prepared ahead, covered and refrigerated for up to 1 hour before baking.

***If sauce breaks down while adding butter, remove from heat. Slowly whisk in 2 tablespoons butter. Once butter has been added, return to low heat and continue as directed above.

NUTRITION INFORMATION PER SERVING
SERVING SIZE: ¼ OF RECIPE SERVED WITH 3 TABLESPOONS SAUCE

		PERCENT U.S. RDA PER SERVING	
Calories	560	Protein	60%
Protein	39 g	Vitamin A	40%
Carbohydrate	39 g	Vitamin C	25%
Fat	26 g	Thiamine	25%
Cholesterol	245 mg	Riboflavin	20%
Sodium	960 mg	Niacin	25%
Potassium	590 mg	Calcium	6%
		Iron	20%

Pear-Walnut Salad

DRESSING
½ cup oil
3 tablespoons white or cider vinegar
¼ cup sugar
½ teaspoon celery seed
¼ teaspoon salt

SALAD
4 cups torn lettuce
1 pear, cored and sliced or chopped
¼ cup toasted walnut halves*
2 ounces blue cheese, crumbled

In jar with tight-fitting lid, combine all dressing ingredients; shake until well blended and sugar is dissolved. Refrigerate to blend flavors. Just before serving, arrange salad ingredients on individual salad plates, or combine all salad ingredients in large bowl. Pour dressing over salad.
4 servings.

TIP: *To toast walnuts, spread on cookie sheet. Bake at 375° F. for 3 to 5 minutes or until golden brown, stirring occasionally. Or spread in thin layer in microwave-safe pie pan. Microwave on HIGH for 3 to 4 minutes or until light golden brown, stirring frequently.

NUTRITION INFORMATION PER SERVING
SERVING SIZE: ¼ OF RECIPE

		PERCENT U.S. RDA PER SERVING	
Calories	430	Protein	6%
Protein	5 g	Vitamin A	6%
Carbohydrate	22 g	Vitamin C	6%
Fat	36 g	Thiamine	4%
Cholesterol	11 mg	Riboflavin	4%
Sodium	340 mg	Niacin	*
Potassium	210 mg	Calcium	10%
		Iron	4%

*Contains less than 2% of the U.S. RDA of this nutrient.

Orange Marjoram Carrots

½ cup water
3 cups sliced fresh carrots
2 tablespoons margarine or butter
1 tablespoon orange juice
1 tablespoon honey
⅛ teaspoon dried marjoram leaves

In medium saucepan, bring water to a boil; add carrots. Cover; simmer 8 to 12 minutes or until carrots are crisp-tender. Drain; stir in margarine, orange juice, honey and marjoram. Cook carrots over low heat until thoroughly heated, stirring constantly.
4 (½-cup) servings.

MICROWAVE DIRECTIONS: In 1½-quart microwave-safe casserole, combine carrots, margarine, orange juice, honey and marjoram; *omit water.* Cover with microwave-safe plastic wrap or glass cover. Microwave on HIGH for 6 to 8 minutes or until carrots are crisp-tender, stirring once halfway through cooking.

NUTRITION INFORMATION PER SERVING
SERVING SIZE: ½ CUP — PERCENT U.S. RDA PER SERVING

Calories	110	Protein	*
Protein	1 g	Vitamin A	520%
Carbohydrate	14 g	Vitamin C	10%
Fat	6 g	Thiamine	6%
Cholesterol	0 mg	Riboflavin	2%
Sodium	100 mg	Niacin	4%
Potassium	310 mg	Calcium	2%
		Iron	2%

*Contains less than 2% of the U.S. RDA of this nutrient.

Apricot-Yogurt Cheesecake

CRUST
½ cup margarine or butter
1 cup all purpose or unbleached flour
½ cup chopped almonds
¼ cup sugar

FILLING
1 envelope unflavored gelatin
1 (16-ounce) can apricot halves, drained, reserving ⅓ cup liquid
½ cup sugar
2 (8-ounce) packages cream cheese, softened
1 (8-ounce) carton plain yogurt
1 teaspoon grated lemon peel

TOPPING
¾ cup apricot preserves
1 to 2 tablespoons Amaretto*

Melt margarine in large skillet over low heat. Stir in remaining crust ingredients. Cook over medium heat until mixture is medium golden brown and crumbly, stirring constantly. Cool slightly; press in bottom of ungreased 9-inch springform pan. Refrigerate until firm.

In small saucepan, combine gelatin and reserved ⅓ cup apricot liquid; let stand 1 minute. Cook over low heat until dissolved, stirring constantly; cool. Meanwhile, puree apricots in food processor bowl with metal blade or in blender. Add ½ cup sugar, cream cheese, yogurt and lemon peel; process until smooth. Carefully stir in gelatin mixture. Pour cream cheese mixture over crust. Refrigerate overnight or until set.

Just before serving, in small saucepan over low heat, heat preserves until softened; stir in Amaretto. Carefully remove sides of springform pan. Drizzle about 1 tablespoon preserves mixture over each serving.
8 to 10 servings.

TIP: *One to 2 tablespoons water and ¼ teaspoon almond extract can be substituted for the Amaretto.

NUTRITION INFORMATION PER SERVING
SERVING SIZE: 1/10 OF RECIPE — PERCENT U.S. RDA PER SERVING

Calories	500	Protein	10%
Protein	8 g	Vitamin A	35%
Carbohydrate	51 g	Vitamin C	2%
Fat	29 g	Thiamine	8%
Cholesterol	51 mg	Riboflavin	15%
Sodium	260 mg	Niacin	6%
Potassium	290 mg	Calcium	10%
		Iron	10%

Special Friends Cappuccino

½ cup instant espresso coffee
2 tablespoons brown sugar
1 cup coffee-flavored liqueur
½ cup Irish cream liqueur
Boiling water
Sweetened whipped cream
Orange zest*

In small bowl, combine espresso, sugar and liqueurs; mix well. Store mix in covered container in refrigerator.

For each serving, spoon 3 tablespoons of mix into small cup; add ½ cup boiling water. Stir to blend. Top with whipped cream and orange zest. Mix can be stored several weeks in refrigerator.
8 (⅔-cup) servings.

TIP: *Orange zest is the colored outer peel of the orange. Remove with citrus zester or vegetable peeler. Cut into strips, if desired.

NUTRITION INFORMATION PER SERVING
SERVING SIZE: ⅔ CUP — PERCENT U.S. RDA PER SERVING

Calories	220	Protein	*
Protein	1 g	Vitamin A	2%
Carbohydrate	35 g	Vitamin C	*
Fat	3 g	Thiamine	*
Cholesterol	10 mg	Riboflavin	*
Sodium	10 mg	Niacin	4%
Potassium	160 mg	Calcium	*
		Iron	*

*Contains less than 2% of the U.S. RDA of this nutrient.

Pictured clockwise from upper left: Tart 'n Tangy Citrus Punch, page 46; Cucumber-Radish Salsa, page 49; Marinated Pork Roast, page 49; Jezebel Sauce, page 49

Bon Voyage Caribbean Buffet

❊

Serves 12

Tropical Rum Punch* Tart 'n Tangy Citrus Punch*
Cheese Turnovers* Coconut-Topped Banana Bread*
Caribbean Spinach Toss* Cucumber-Radish Salsa*
Marinated Pork Roast* Jezebel Sauce*
Ginger Rice Medley* Cou-Cou*
Tropical Lime Ice Cream Dessert*
Coffee Tea

*Recipe included

---

*I*sland breezes beckon with a lively culinary celebration of exotic food and drink. Use this tropical theme for a going-away party for globe-trotting friends, as a toast to a twenty-fifth or other milestone wedding anniversary, to honor a retiree with travel in the offing, or as a passport to sun and warmth when snow is piled high outside your door. It won't take long for guests to get in the swing of a calypso beat if they are encouraged to appear in Caribbean attire.

You may not be able to re-create the seductive climate of this tourist mecca, but you certainly can capture the festive atmosphere. Set the scene for your own special feast day by decorating with straw hats, baskets and mats accented with splashes of color from tropical flowers, yardage of island print fabrics and bright pottery. A centerpiece of pineapples and other fresh fruits or a grouping of shells will enhance the Caribbean ambiance. A little island music in the background, Maestro, and your party is ready to enjoy.

Preparation Timetable

Several Days Ahead

Prepare *Tropical Lime Ice Cream Dessert;* cover and freeze • Prepare ice ring for *Tart 'n Tangy Citrus Punch* • Prepare *Jezebel Sauce;* cover and refrigerate.

Day Before Buffet

Place concentrates in refrigerator to thaw; refrigerate juices and sodas for punches • Prepare *Cucumber-Radish Salsa;* cover and refrigerate • Prepare *Coconut-Topped Banana Bread;* cool, wrap and refrigerate • Marinate meat in refrigerator for *Marinated Pork Roast.*

Day of Buffet

Early in the Day: Prepare dressing, wash spinach and cut up fruit and vegetables, except avocados, for *Caribbean Spinach Toss;* cover and refrigerate •

Several Hours Before: Roast pork • Prepare *Cheese Turnovers* but do not fry; cover and refrigerate • About 1 hour before serving, prepare *Cou-Cou.*

Shortly Before Serving: Complete preparation of punches • Fry turnovers • Slice avocados; complete preparation of spinach toss • Prepare *Ginger Rice Medley* • Prepare coffee and/or tea • About 10 minutes before serving, remove dessert from freezer to soften for easier cutting.

Tropical Rum Punch

1 (46-ounce) can (5¾ cups) pineapple juice, chilled
1 (6-ounce) can frozen limeade concentrate, thawed
1½ to 2 cups rum
1 (1-liter) bottle (4¼ cups) club soda, chilled
Dash Angostura bitters

In large nonmetal pitcher or punch bowl, combine pineapple juice, limeade concentrate and rum; mix well. Refrigerate until thoroughly chilled. Just before serving, stir in club soda and bitters. Garnish each serving with wedge of fresh pineapple and maraschino cherry, if desired.
24 (½-cup) servings.

NUTRITION INFORMATION PER SERVING

SERVING SIZE: ½ CUP		PERCENT U.S. RDA PER SERVING	
Calories	90	Protein	*
Protein	0 g	Vitamin A	*
Carbohydrate	13 g	Vitamin C	10%
Fat	0 g	Thiamine	2%
Cholesterol	0 mg	Riboflavin	*
Sodium	10 mg	Niacin	*
Potassium	85 mg	Calcium	*
		Iron	*

*Contains less than 2% of the U.S. RDA of this nutrient.

Tart 'n Tangy Citrus Punch

1 (6-ounce) can frozen lemonade concentrate, thawed
1 (6-ounce) can frozen grapefruit juice concentrate, thawed
1 (6-ounce) can frozen pineapple juice concentrate, thawed
2 cups water
1 (1-liter) bottle (4¼ cups) club soda, chilled
1 (1-liter) bottle (4¼ cups) ginger ale, chilled
Ice ring or ice mold, if desired
Fresh fruit slices, if desired

In large nonmetal pitcher or punch bowl, combine concentrates and water; mix well. Refrigerate until thoroughly chilled. Just before serving, stir in club soda and ginger ale. Garnish punch bowl with ice ring and fresh fruit slices.
25 (½-cup) servings.

NUTRITION INFORMATION PER SERVING

SERVING SIZE: ½ CUP		PERCENT U.S. RDA PER SERVING	
Calories	60	Protein	*
Protein	0 g	Vitamin A	*
Carbohydrate	15 g	Vitamin C	30%
Fat	0 g	Thiamine	2%
Cholesterol	0 mg	Riboflavin	*
Sodium	10 mg	Niacin	*
Potassium	100 mg	Calcium	*
		Iron	*

*Contains less than 2% of the U.S. RDA of this nutrient.

Caribbean Spinach Toss

DRESSING
½ cup oil
¼ cup lemon juice
2 tablespoons chopped fresh parsley
1 teaspoon sugar
½ teaspoon salt
½ teaspoon grated fresh gingerroot

SALAD
8 cups torn spinach leaves
3 medium tomatoes, cut into wedges
2 cups fresh pineapple chunks
1 (14-ounce) can hearts of palm, drained, cut into 1-inch pieces
½ cup chopped red onion
2 medium avocados, peeled, thinly sliced*

In jar with tight-fitting lid, combine all dressing ingredients; shake well. Refrigerate to blend flavors. In very large salad bowl, combine all salad ingredients. Pour dressing over salad; toss gently.
12 servings.

TIP: *Dip avocado slices in lemon juice to prevent discoloration, if desired.

NUTRITION INFORMATION PER SERVING

SERVING SIZE: 1/12 OF RECIPE		PERCENT U.S. RDA PER SERVING	
Calories	210	Protein	4%
Protein	3 g	Vitamin A	60%
Carbohydrate	16 g	Vitamin C	45%
Fat	15 g	Thiamine	8%
Cholesterol	0 mg	Riboflavin	10%
Sodium	130 mg	Niacin	6%
Potassium	940 mg	Calcium	4%
		Iron	10%

Ginger Rice Medley

4 (10-ounce) packages frozen long-grain rice with peas and mushrooms in a pouch
1 tablespoon grated fresh gingerroot

In large Dutch oven, place unopened rice pouches in vigorously boiling water. DO NOT COVER. Bring water to a second vigorous boil and heat for 12 minutes, turning pouches over halfway through heating time. Cut or tear pouches open; place in large serving dish. Add gingerroot; toss gently.
12 servings.

NUTRITION INFORMATION PER SERVING

SERVING SIZE: 1/12 OF RECIPE		PERCENT U.S. RDA PER SERVING	
Calories	80	Protein	2%
Protein	2 g	Vitamin A	*
Carbohydrate	16 g	Vitamin C	2%
Fat	1 g	Thiamine	10%
Cholesterol	0 mg	Riboflavin	*
Sodium	260 mg	Niacin	8%
Potassium	50 mg	Calcium	*
		Iron	2%

*Contains less than 2% of the U.S. RDA of this nutrient.

Cheese Turnovers

Cou-Cou

1 cup water
½ teaspoon dried oregano leaves
1 (10-ounce) package frozen cut okra
2 cups cornmeal
2 cups cold water
¼ cup margarine or butter
1½ teaspoons salt

Heat oven to 350° F. Grease 2-quart casserole. In medium saucepan, bring 1 cup water and oregano to a boil; add okra. Cover; simmer about 8 minutes or until okra is crisp-tender. Do not drain.

In medium bowl, combine cornmeal and 2 cups cold water; mix well. Gradually add to okra, stirring constantly. Cook over medium heat for 2 to 3 minutes or until mixture thickens, stirring occasionally. Stir in margarine and salt. Pour into greased casserole. Bake at 350° F. for 30 to 45 minutes or until set. Invert onto serving plate. Serve with additional margarine, if desired.
12 servings.

NUTRITION INFORMATION PER SERVING
SERVING SIZE: 1/12 OF   PERCENT U.S. RDA PER
RECIPE   SERVING

Calories	120	Protein	2%
Protein	2 g	Vitamin A	6%
Carbohydrate	17 g	Vitamin C	2%
Fat	5 g	Thiamine	6%
Cholesterol	0 mg	Riboflavin	4%
Sodium	320 mg	Niacin	4%
Potassium	110 mg	Calcium	2%
		Iron	4%

Cheese Turnovers

2 (7.5-ounce) cans refrigerated buttermilk
   biscuits
2 ounces Edam cheese, cut into 20 pieces
   Oil for deep frying
   Powdered sugar

Separate dough into 20 biscuits. Press or roll out each to a 3-inch circle. Place 1 piece of cheese on each circle. Fold dough in half over cheese, completely covering cheese; pinch edges firmly to seal. (At this point, turnovers can be covered and refrigerated for up to 2 hours.)

In deep fryer or heavy saucepan, heat 2 to 3 inches of oil to 350° F. Fry turnovers until golden brown, about 1 minute on each side. Drain on paper towels. Dust with powdered sugar. Serve warm.
20 turnovers.

NUTRITION INFORMATION PER SERVING
SERVING SIZE: 1   PERCENT U.S. RDA PER
TURNOVER   SERVING

Calories	80	Protein	2%
Protein	2 g	Vitamin A	*
Carbohydrate	10 g	Vitamin C	*
Fat	3 g	Thiamine	4%
Cholesterol	3 mg	Riboflavin	4%
Sodium	210 mg	Niacin	2%
Potassium	110 mg	Calcium	2%
		Iron	2%

*Contains less than 2% of the U.S. RDA of this nutrient.

Pictured from top: Coconut-Topped Banana Bread; Ginger Rice Medley, page 46

Coconut-Topped Banana Bread

BREAD
  1 package banana bread mix
  1 cup water
  3 tablespoons oil
  2 eggs
  ½ cup coconut

TOPPING
  ¼ cup coconut
  1 tablespoon margarine or butter, melted

Heat oven to 375° F. Grease and flour bottom only of 8 × 4- or 9 × 5-inch loaf pan. In large bowl, combine all bread ingredients; stir 50 to 75 strokes until dry particles are moistened. Pour into greased pan. In small bowl, combine topping ingredients; mix well. Sprinkle over top of bread mixture.

Bake at 375° F. for 40 to 50 minutes or until toothpick inserted in center comes out clean. Cool 15 minutes; remove from pan. Cool completely. Wrap tightly; store in refrigerator.
1 (16-slice) loaf.

HIGH ALTITUDE—Above 3500 Feet: Add 2 tablespoons flour to dry bread mix.

NUTRITION INFORMATION PER SERVING
SERVING SIZE: 1 SLICE

		PERCENT U.S. RDA PER SERVING	
Calories	150	Protein	2%
Protein	2 g	Vitamin A	*
Carbohydrate	23 g	Vitamin C	*
Fat	6 g	Thiamine	6%
Cholesterol	27 mg	Riboflavin	4%
Sodium	170 mg	Niacin	2%
Potassium	35 mg	Calcium	*
		Iron	2%

*Contains less than 2% of the U.S. RDA of this nutrient.

Marinated Pork Roast

1 cup soy sauce
2 tablespoons lemon juice
1 tablespoon finely chopped garlic
1 tablespoon chopped fresh chives or 1
   teaspoon dried chives
2 teaspoons dried tarragon leaves
2 teaspoons dried basil leaves
1 teaspoon ground sage
1 teaspoon pepper
1 (3 to 4-pound) boneless pork loin roast

In small bowl, combine all ingredients except
pork roast; mix well. Place pork in plastic bag or
nonmetal bowl. Pour marinade mixture over
pork. Seal bag or cover bowl. Marinate 2 to 3
hours at room temperature or overnight in
refrigerator, turning pork several times.

Heat oven to 325° F. Remove pork from
marinade; reserve marinade. Place pork in
shallow roasting pan. Insert meat thermometer
into center of thickest part of meat, being careful
bulb does not rest on fat. Roast at 325° F. for 1½
to 2½ hours or until meat thermometer reaches
165° F., basting with marinade every 30 minutes.
Let stand 15 minutes before slicing.
12 servings.

NUTRITION INFORMATION PER SERVING
SERVING SIZE: ½₁₂ OF RECIPE

		PERCENT U.S. RDA PER SERVING	
Calories	290	Protein	50%
Protein	32 g	Vitamin A	*
Carbohydrate	1 g	Vitamin C	*
Fat	17 g	Thiamine	60%
Cholesterol	107 mg	Riboflavin	25%
Sodium	430 mg	Niacin	35%
Potassium	450 mg	Calcium	*
		Iron	8%

*Contains less than 2% of the U.S. RDA of this nutrient.

Jezebel Sauce

1 (12-ounce) jar pineapple preserves
1 (10-ounce) jar apple jelly
4 tablespoons Dijon mustard
2 tablespoons prepared horseradish

In small bowl, combine all ingredients; mix well.
Cover; store in refrigerator. Serve as condiment
with pork roast.
2½ cups.

NUTRITION INFORMATION PER SERVING
SERVING SIZE: 1 TABLESPOON

		PERCENT U.S. RDA PER SERVING	
Calories	45	Protein	*
Protein	0 g	Vitamin A	*
Carbohydrate	11 g	Vitamin C	2%
Fat	0 g	Thiamine	*
Cholesterol	0 mg	Riboflavin	*
Sodium	45 mg	Niacin	*
Potassium	15 mg	Calcium	*
		Iron	*

*Contains less than 2% of the U.S. RDA of this nutrient.

Cucumber-Radish Salsa

2 medium cucumbers, seeded, finely chopped
6 radishes, finely chopped
1 garlic clove, finely chopped
2 tablespoons white or cider vinegar
1½ to 3 teaspoons finely chopped fresh hot chile
   peppers*
¼ teaspoon salt

In medium bowl, combine all ingredients; mix
well. Cover; refrigerate at least 1 hour or
overnight to blend flavors. Serve as condiment
with pork roast. **3 cups.**

TIP: *Hot chile peppers must be handled
carefully. Wear rubber gloves and keep hands
away from eyes.

NUTRITION INFORMATION PER SERVING
SERVING SIZE: ¼ CUP

		PERCENT U.S. RDA PER SERVING	
Calories	6	Protein	*
Protein	0 g	Vitamin A	2%
Carbohydrate	1 g	Vitamin C	4%
Fat	0 g	Thiamine	*
Cholesterol	0 mg	Riboflavin	*
Sodium	55 mg	Niacin	*
Potassium	65 mg	Calcium	*
		Iron	*

*Contains less than 2% of the U.S. RDA of this nutrient.

Tropical Lime Ice Cream Dessert

CRUST
2 cups crisp coconut cookie crumbs
⅓ cup margarine or butter, melted

FILLING
1 quart (4 cups) lime sherbet, softened
1 (8-ounce) can crushed pineapple, drained
1 quart (4 cups) vanilla ice cream, softened
1 teaspoon grated lime peel, if desired

In medium bowl, combine crust ingredients; mix
well. Reserve 3 tablespoons crumb mixture for
topping. Press remaining crumb mixture lightly
in bottom of ungreased 13 × 9-inch pan.

Spoon sherbet into crust-lined pan; top with
pineapple. Spread ice cream over pineapple. Top
with reserved crumb mixture and lime peel.
Freeze until firm. Let stand at room temperature
about 10 minutes before serving.
12 servings.

NUTRITION INFORMATION PER SERVING
SERVING SIZE: ½₁₂ OF RECIPE

		PERCENT U.S. RDA PER SERVING	
Calories	330	Protein	4%
Protein	3 g	Vitamin A	8%
Carbohydrate	44 g	Vitamin C	4%
Fat	16 g	Thiamine	2%
Cholesterol	45 mg	Riboflavin	10%
Sodium	135 mg	Niacin	*
Potassium	270 mg	Calcium	10%
		Iron	2%

*Contains less than 2% of the U.S. RDA of this nutrient.

Pictured clockwise from lower left: Roasted Pepper and Pasta Salad, page 52; Whole Wheat Zucchini Bars, page 53; Sour Cream and Onion Loaves, pages 52–53

Retirement Office Party

Serves 12
Chilled Flavored Sparkling Waters
Layered Chef's Salad with Herbed Mayonnaise*
Fresh Fruit Combo with Orange Dressing*
Roasted Pepper and Pasta Salad*
Sour Cream and Onion Loaves*
Whole Wheat Zucchini Bars*   Almost Candy Bars*
Coffee   Tea
*Recipe included

*R*etirement can be a bittersweet benchmark. As a complete change of pace to a formal luncheon or dinner, try a potluck office party. In this informal atmosphere, everyone has the pleasure of making a tangible contribution and all participants have ample opportunity to express their best wishes to the retiree.

Planning is almost effortless; assign culinary and other tasks and reserve a conference room or section of the employee lunchroom for the setting. Those who enjoy cooking can sign up to prepare one or more of the tasty totables, all of which are prepared the day before the party. Non-cooks can volunteer to bring non-edibles like plates, cups, flatware, serving pieces, etc. and can lend a hand with the minimal tasks of setting up and cleanup.

If your office does not have a refrigerator, keep the salads in coolers until lunchtime. Slicing the loaves simplifies serving and bars can be cut in advance and arranged on a pretty platter for easy pickup. The office gardener might enjoy contributing a freshly cut bouquet for the buffet table centerpiece. Or, for a touch of welcome greenery, create a grouping of plants from various offices.

Once the table is laid, people can help themselves beginning with the guest of honor. All foods are planned for easy eating to encourage mingling. It will be the relaxed atmosphere, home-prepared foods and personal exchanges that will make this milestone memorable for everyone present.

Preparation Timetable

Day Before Party

Refrigerate flavored sparkling waters • Prepare *Layered Chef's Salad with Herbed Mayonnaise, Fresh Fruit Combo with Orange Dressing, Roasted Pepper and Pasta Salad;* cover and refrigerate. • Prepare *Sour Cream and Onion Loaves;* cool completely, place in plastic bags and store at room temperature • Prepare *Whole Wheat Zucchini Bars* and *Almost Candy Bars;* cover and store at room temperature.

Shortly Before Serving

Prepare coffee and/or tea • Slice onion loaves.

Layered Chef's Salad with Herbed Mayonnaise

1 cup mayonnaise
3 tablespoons prepared Italian dressing
4 cups torn iceberg lettuce
½ cup chopped onion
1 cup diced radishes
1 cup halved cherry tomatoes
1 cup chopped celery
8 ounces (2 cups) shredded Cheddar cheese
2 cups cubed cooked chicken or turkey
4 slices bacon, crisply cooked, crumbled

In small bowl, combine mayonnaise and Italian dressing. In 2½-quart bowl or 13 × 9-inch pan, layer lettuce, onion, radishes, tomatoes and celery; top with dressing. Sprinkle with 1½ cups of the cheese. Top with chicken and remaining ½ cup cheese; sprinkle with bacon pieces. Cover; refrigerate at least 8 hours so that dressing can blend thoroughly with ingredients before serving.
12 (¾-cup) servings.

NUTRITION INFORMATION PER SERVING
SERVING SIZE: ¾ CUP

		PERCENT U.S. RDA PER SERVING	
Calories	300	Protein	20%
Protein	13 g	Vitamin A	8%
Carbohydrate	3 g	Vitamin C	10%
Fat	26 g	Thiamine	4%
Cholesterol	53 mg	Riboflavin	8%
Sodium	320 mg	Niacin	10%
Potassium	210 mg	Calcium	15%
		Iron	4%

Fresh Fruit Combo with Orange Dressing

3 cups cantaloupe balls or cubes
3 cups fresh pineapple chunks
2 cups halved fresh strawberries

DRESSING
¼ cup orange marmalade
2 tablespoons lemon juice
2 tablespoons orange-flavored liqueur or orange juice

In large bowl, combine fruits; toss gently. In small bowl, combine all dressing ingredients; mix well. Pour dressing over fruit mixture; stir to coat completely. Cover; refrigerate several hours or overnight to blend flavors, stirring once.
16 (½-cup) servings.

NUTRITION INFORMATION PER SERVING
SERVING SIZE: ½ CUP

		PERCENT U.S. RDA PER SERVING	
Calories	50	Protein	*
Protein	1 g	Vitamin A	20%
Carbohydrate	13 g	Vitamin C	50%
Fat	0 g	Thiamine	2%
Cholesterol	0 mg	Riboflavin	*
Sodium	0 mg	Niacin	*
Potassium	170 mg	Calcium	*
		Iron	*

*Contains less than 2% of the U.S. RDA of this nutrient.

Roasted Pepper and Pasta Salad

1 medium red bell pepper, seeded, cut into fourths
6½ ounces (2 cups) uncooked rotini (spiral macaroni)
2 cups fresh spinach, cut into thin strips
1 cup (1 medium) sliced zucchini
½ cup (1 medium) thinly sliced carrot
½ cup prepared Italian dressing
2 tablespoons chopped fresh parsley
2 tablespoons lemon juice
1 teaspoon grated lemon peel

Place red pepper quarters on broiler pan skin side up. Broil 3 to 4 inches from heat until skin blackens. Remove from broiler and place in plastic bag; let stand 10 minutes to steam. Peel skin from pepper; cut pepper into ½-inch pieces.

Cook rotini to desired doneness as directed on package. Drain; rinse with cold water. In large bowl, combine all ingredients. Cover; refrigerate several hours or overnight.
14 (½-cup) servings.

NUTRITION INFORMATION PER SERVING
SERVING SIZE: ½ CUP

		PERCENT U.S. RDA PER SERVING	
Calories	100	Protein	2%
Protein	2 g	Vitamin A	45%
Carbohydrate	12 g	Vitamin C	25%
Fat	4 g	Thiamine	10%
Cholesterol	0 mg	Riboflavin	4%
Sodium	75 mg	Niacin	6%
Potassium	120 mg	Calcium	*
		Iron	4%

*Contains less than 2% of the U.S. RDA of this nutrient.

Sour Cream and Onion Loaves

1 cup chopped onions
1 tablespoon butter or margarine
1 package hot roll mix
¾ cup water heated to 120 to 130° F.
½ cup dairy sour cream
1 egg, beaten
Poppy seed

Grease 2 cookie sheets. In small saucepan, cook onions in butter until tender; reserve ¼ of onions for topping. In large bowl, combine flour mixture with yeast from foil packet; blend well. Stir in *hot* water, sour cream and remaining ¾ of the onions until dough pulls away from sides of bowl. Turn dough out onto lightly floured surface. With greased or floured hands, shape dough into a ball. Knead dough for 5 minutes until smooth. Cover with large bowl; let rest 5 minutes.

On lightly floured surface, divide dough into 4 equal pieces. Shape each piece into 6-inch oblong loaf. Place loaves 4 to 6 inches apart on greased cookie sheets. Using sharp knife, make a 5-inch slash lengthwise down center of each loaf, cutting about ½ inch deep. Carefully brush tops of loaves with beaten egg. Spoon ¼ of reserved onions into each slash; sprinkle tops of loaves with poppy seed. Cover loosely with greased plastic wrap and cloth towel. Let rise in warm place (80 to 85° F.) for 30 minutes.

Heat oven to 375° F. Uncover dough. Bake at 375° F. for 20 to 25 minutes or until loaves sound hollow when lightly tapped. Cool completely.
4 (7-slice) loaves.

HIGH ALTITUDE—Above 3500 Feet: No change.

NUTRITION INFORMATION PER SERVING
SERVING SIZE: 1 SLICE PERCENT U.S. RDA PER SERVING

Calories	80	Protein	2%
Protein	2 g	Vitamin A	*
Carbohydrate	13 g	Vitamin C	*
Fat	2 g	Thiamine	8%
Cholesterol	11 mg	Riboflavin	6%
Sodium	120 mg	Niacin	4%
Potassium	40 mg	Calcium	*
		Iron	2%

*Contains less than 2% of the U.S. RDA of this nutrient.

Almost Candy Bars

¾ cup margarine or butter
1 package pudding-included devil's food cake mix
1 (6-ounce) package (1 cup) butterscotch chips
1 (6-ounce) package (1 cup) semi-sweet chocolate chips
1 cup coconut
1 cup chopped nuts
1 (14-ounce) can sweetened condensed milk (not evaporated)

Heat oven to 350° F. In large bowl, cut margarine into cake mix with fork or pastry blender until crumbly. Sprinkle evenly over bottom of 15 × 10 × 1-inch baking pan; press lightly. Sprinkle with butterscotch chips, chocolate chips, coconut and nuts. Pour sweetened condensed milk over all ingredients. Bake at 350° F. for 20 to 30 minutes or until light golden brown. Cool completely. Cut into bars.
48 bars.

HIGH ALTITUDE—Above 3500 Feet: No change.

NUTRITION INFORMATION PER SERVING
SERVING SIZE: 1 BAR PERCENT U.S. RDA PER SERVING

Calories	160	Protein	2%
Protein	2 g	Vitamin A	2%
Carbohydrate	19 g	Vitamin C	*
Fat	9 g	Thiamine	2%
Cholesterol	4 mg	Riboflavin	4%
Sodium	130 mg	Niacin	*
Potassium	115 mg	Calcium	6%
		Iron	2%

*Contains less than 2% of the U.S. RDA of this nutrient.

Whole Wheat Zucchini Bars

BARS
3 eggs
1½ cups sugar
1 cup oil
1½ cups whole wheat flour
½ cup all purpose or unbleached flour
1 teaspoon baking powder
½ teaspoon salt
1 teaspoon cinnamon
2 cups shredded zucchini
1 cups currants or raisins

GLAZE
1 cup powdered sugar
¼ teaspoon cinnamon
2 tablespoons margarine or butter, melted
2 tablespoons milk

Heat oven to 350° F. Grease 13 × 9-inch pan. In large bowl, beat eggs. Add sugar and oil; beat well. Lightly spoon flour into measuring cup; level off. In medium bowl, combine whole wheat flour, all purpose flour, baking powder, salt and 1 teaspoon cinnamon. Add flour mixture to egg mixture; mix well. Stir in zucchini and currants. Spread in greased pan. Bake at 350° F. for 40 to 50 minutes or until toothpick inserted in center comes out clean. Cool completely.

In small bowl, combine all glaze ingredients until smooth. Spread evenly over cooled bars. Cut into bars.
36 bars.

HIGH ALTITUDE—Above 3500 Feet: No change.

NUTRITION INFORMATION PER SERVING
SERVING SIZE: 1 BAR PERCENT U.S. RDA PER SERVING

Calories	140	Protein	2%
Protein	2 g	Vitamin A	*
Carbohydrate	17 g	Vitamin C	6%
Fat	7 g	Thiamine	2%
Cholesterol	18 mg	Riboflavin	2%
Sodium	50 mg	Niacin	2%
Potassium	60 mg	Calcium	*
		Iron	2%

*Contains less than 2% of the U.S. RDA of this nutrient.

Pictured clockwise from left: Cookie and Cone Clowns, page 62; Wheel-o'-Fun Cakes, page 89; Party-a-Saurus Cake, pages 76–77

Birthday
Celebrations

What to give the person who has everything? A birthday party, of course. What gift could be more personal and meaningful than a unique celebration specifically planned to honor a significant day in each person's life? Few celebrations offer more opportunity for creativity.

This section includes parties for all ages beginning with the very young. Many of the menus are quite simple to prepare and yet each offers some distinctive recipes and decorating ideas for making memories. Don't be surprised if ten years down the road your former Little Leaguer still recalls with fondness the All-Star Cookie Treat. Teens will delight in the casual ambiance of the '90s style Video Party just as a friend or relative will relish the benchmark birthday fete that puts him or her in the spotlight.

When planning a birthday party, there are three particularly important considerations—the honoree's age, interests and preferences. Lively youngsters require adequate supervision, games suited to their ages and skills, endurance levels and attention spans plus a menu featuring familiar and easily handled foods. For an adult, you will get high marks for building a theme around the celebrant's interests and personal tastes. For example, the outdoor, laid-back type probably will be most comfortable with a less sophisticated approach. In contrast, one whose tastes encompass elegant, formal settings is apt to favor fancier embellishments. However, whatever menu and theme you select, the most important ingredient is FUN. And that's what these menus are all about!

Baby Block Cakes, page 59

Baby Blocks Birthday Party

Serves 12
Chilled Apple Juice and Flavored Sparkling Waters
Confetti Fruit Salad†
Butter Crumb Breadsticks*
Seafood Vegetable Bake*
Mom's Goulash*
Pastel Coconut Ice Cream Balls*
Baby Block Cakes*
Coffee   Tea
*Recipe included

*T*he toddler being honored on a first, second or third birthday may not understand what the fuss is about. But he or she is certain to enjoy all the excitement—relatives and friends to share a special supper, balloons and other party favors, candles to blow out and wonderful presents to open.

Since Mom and Dad are going to be busy keeping an eye on the little ones, an almost totally make-ahead menu is essential. Except for the Butter Crumb Breadsticks, which are prepared just before serving, the dishes can be assembled hours ahead, covered and refrigerated until serving or baking time. Two different casseroles will suit the appetites of all ages. Mom's Goulash will be met with raves from the guest of honor and young guests, while adults will savor the rich Seafood Vegetable Bake. And, oh what wonders are wrought with a cake mix! These adorable Baby Block Cakes result from just minutes of effort and creativity. Remember this simple method of preparing petits fours for teas and other, more formal, occasions too. Just alter tint and decorations to suit color scheme and occasion.

Because small children find prolonged activity exhausting and delayed eating frustrating, gifts can be opened while the food is being heated. By the time the last cake crumb is consumed, it will be time for a nap or a good night's sleep for the younger set. It's always more pleasant to end the party while everyone is still smiling.

Preparation Timetable

Day Before Party
Refrigerate apple juice and flavored sparkling waters • Prepare *Pastel Coconut Ice Cream Balls;* freeze until firm, cover with plastic wrap and return to freezer.

Day of Party
Early in the Day: • Prepare *Baby Block Cakes;* cover loosely and store at room temperature.

Several Hours Before: Prepare *Seafood Vegetable Bake* and *Mom's Goulash,* but do not bake; cover with foil and refrigerate • Prepare *Confetti Fruit Salad,* doubled, page 74; cover and refrigerate.

Shortly Before Serving: Prepare *Butter Crumb Breadsticks;* keep warm • Uncover goulash; bake, allowing extra baking time due to refrigeration • About 40 minutes before serving, bake foil-covered seafood casserole • Prepare coffee and/or tea.

†Double recipe on page 74.

Seafood Vegetable Bake

8 ounces (2½ cups) uncooked rotini (spiral
    macaroni)
3 tablespoons margarine or butter
1 cup julienne-cut carrots
1 garlic clove, minced
1 cup thinly sliced zucchini
1 (9-ounce) package frozen cut broccoli in a
    pouch, thawed
1 teaspoon seasoned salt or salt

SAUCE
  2 cups half-and-half or milk
  3 tablespoons flour
  ½ teaspoon dried dill weed
  ¼ teaspoon salt
  3 tablespoons grated Parmesan cheese
  2 tablespoons dry white wine
  1 (10-ounce) package frozen cooked large
    shrimp, thawed and rinsed, or 1 (12-
    ounce) package frozen imitation crab legs,
    thawed, rinsed, cut into chunks

Grease 13 × 9-inch (3-quart) baking dish. Cook
rotini to desired doneness as directed on package.
Drain; rinse with hot water. Place in bottom of
greased dish.

Heat oven to 350° F. Melt margarine in large
skillet over medium heat. Add carrots and garlic;
cook 2 minutes, stirring occasionally. Add
zucchini and broccoli; cook and stir an additional
2 minutes. Sprinkle with seasoned salt; stir well.
Reserve ½ cup of cooked vegetables; set aside.
Spoon remaining cooked vegetables over rotini.

In small bowl, combine half-and-half, flour, dill
weed and salt; blend well using wire whisk. Pour
into same skillet. Cook over medium heat until
mixture boils and thickens, stirring constantly.
Remove from heat; stir in Parmesan cheese, wine
and shrimp. Spoon sauce mixture evenly over
vegetables. Top with reserved vegetables; cover
with foil. Bake at 350° F. for 25 to 30 minutes or
until hot and bubbly.
8 (1-cup) servings.

NUTRITION INFORMATION PER SERVING
SERVING SIZE: 1 CUP   PERCENT U.S. RDA PER
                                  SERVING

Calories	300	Protein	25%
Protein	15 g	Vitamin A	100%
Carbohydrate	30 g	Vitamin C	20%
Fat	13 g	Thiamine	25%
Cholesterol	93 mg	Riboflavin	15%
Sodium	540 mg	Niacin	15%
Potassium	330 mg	Calcium	15%
		Iron	15%

Mom's Goulash

8 ounces (2½ cups) uncooked rotini (spiral
    macaroni)
1 pound ground beef
1½ cups chopped celery
1 medium onion, chopped
1 teaspoon dried basil leaves
½ teaspoon salt
¼ teaspoon pepper
1 (10¾-ounce) can condensed tomato soup
1 (28-ounce) can (3 cups) whole tomatoes,
    undrained, cut up

Cook rotini to desired doneness as directed on
package. Drain; rinse with hot water. Set aside.

Heat oven to 350° F. In Dutch oven over
medium-high heat, brown ground beef, celery
and onion; drain well. Add remaining ingredients
except rotini; heat thoroughly. Stir in rotini; pour
into ungreased 3-quart casserole. Bake at 350° F.
for 45 minutes or until thoroughly heated.
8 (1-cup) servings.

NUTRITION INFORMATION PER SERVING
SERVING SIZE: 1 CUP   PERCENT U.S. RDA PER
                                  SERVING

Calories	200	Protein	20%
Protein	13 g	Vitamin A	15%
Carbohydrate	18 g	Vitamin C	45%
Fat	9 g	Thiamine	10%
Cholesterol	46 mg	Riboflavin	10%
Sodium	640 mg	Niacin	20%
Potassium	510 mg	Calcium	4%
		Iron	15%

Butter Crumb Breadsticks

10 buttery round crackers, crushed
1 tablespoon grated Parmesan cheese
1 teaspoon parsley flakes
1 (11-ounce) can refrigerated breadsticks
1 tablespoon margarine or butter, melted

Heat oven to 350° F. In small bowl, combine
crushed crackers, Parmesan cheese and parsley
flakes. Unroll dough; separate at perforations to
form 8 strips. Cut each strip in half crosswise;
twist on flat surface. Place 1 inch apart on 1 large
or 2 small ungreased cookie sheets. Press ends
down firmly on cookie sheet. Brush each
breadstick with margarine; sprinkle evenly with
cracker mixture. Bake at 350° F. for 14 to 16
minutes or until golden brown. Serve warm.
16 breadsticks.

NUTRITION INFORMATION PER SERVING
SERVING SIZE: 1   PERCENT U.S. RDA PER
BREADSTICK   SERVING

Calories	70	Protein	2%
Protein	2 g	Vitamin A	*
Carbohydrate	10 g	Vitamin C	*
Fat	2 g	Thiamine	50%
Cholesterol	0 mg	Riboflavin	2%
Sodium	150 mg	Niacin	2%
Potassium	15 mg	Calcium	*
		Iron	2%

*Contains less than 2% of the U.S. RDA of this nutrient.

Baby Block Cakes

CAKE
1 package pudding-included white cake mix
   with candy bits*
¾ cup water
½ cup dairy sour cream
2 eggs

ICING
6 cups powdered sugar
½ cup water
⅓ cup light corn syrup
¼ cup margarine or butter, melted
1 teaspoon vanilla
½ teaspoon almond extract
   Frosting, tinted desired color
   Decorating bag and tips
   Assorted decorative candies

Heat oven to 350° F. Grease 13 × 9-inch pan; line
with waxed paper and grease again. In large
bowl, combine cake mix, ¾ cup water, sour cream
and eggs at low speed until moistened; beat 2
minutes at high speed. Fold in candy sprinkles.
Pour into greased and lined pan. Bake at 350° F.
for 30 to 40 minutes or until toothpick inserted
in center comes out clean. Cool 10 minutes;
carefully remove cake from pan. Remove waxed
paper from cake; cool completely.

If necessary, trim cake to obtain straight sides and
level top. Cut cake lengthwise into 4 equal strips.
Cut each strip into 6 equal pieces, forming 24
blocks. In large bowl, combine all icing
ingredients; blend at low speed until powdered
sugar is moistened. Beat at high speed until
smooth. If necessary, add 2 to 3 teaspoons water
until icing is of desired drizzling consistency.

Set cake blocks on wire rack over 15 × 10 × 1-inch
baking pan or waxed paper. Spoon icing evenly
over top and sides of cake pieces. (Icing that drips
off can be reused.) Allow icing to set. Using
tinted frosting, decorating bag, tips and candies,
decorate cakes to resemble children's building
blocks.
24 cakes.

TIP: *If desired, 1 package pudding-included
white cake mix can be substituted; fold in ¼ cup
multicolored candy sprinkles.

HIGH ALTITUDE—Above 3500 Feet: Add 2
tablespoons flour to dry cake mix. Bake as
directed above.

NUTRITION INFORMATION PER SERVING
SERVING SIZE: 1 CAKE

		PERCENT U.S. RDA PER SERVING	
Calories	260	Protein	2%
Protein	2 g	Vitamin A	2%
Carbohydrate	49 g	Vitamin C	*
Fat	6 g	Thiamine	2%
Cholesterol	20 mg	Riboflavin	2%
Sodium	160 mg	Niacin	2%
Potassium	25 mg	Calcium	4%
		Iron	2%

*Contains less than 2% of the U.S. RDA of this nutrient.

Pastel Coconut Ice Cream Balls

3 cups flaked coconut
   Red, blue, green and yellow food coloring
½ gallon (8 cups) vanilla ice cream

Line large cookie sheet with waxed paper. Place
¾ cup of the coconut in each of 4 plastic bags.
Add 2 to 3 drops red, blue, green or yellow food
coloring and 2 to 3 drops water to each bag; close
bag. Shake coconut until desired color is reached.
Using ½-cup ice cream scoop, shape ice cream
into 16 balls. Place on paper-lined cookie sheet;
freeze until firm.

Empty each bag of tinted coconut onto a separate
sheet of waxed paper. Remove ice cream balls
from freezer. Working quickly, roll each ball in
desired color of coconut; return to cookie sheet.
Freeze until firm.
16 servings.

NUTRITION INFORMATION PER SERVING
SERVING SIZE: 1/16 OF RECIPE

		PERCENT U.S. RDA PER SERVING	
Calories	210	Protein	4%
Protein	3 g	Vitamin A	4%
Carbohydrate	22 g	Vitamin C	*
Fat	12 g	Thiamine	2%
Cholesterol	30 mg	Riboflavin	10%
Sodium	60 mg	Niacin	*
Potassium	180 mg	Calcium	8%
		Iron	*

*Contains less than 2% of the U.S. RDA of this nutrient.

Cookie and Cone Clowns, page 62

Clown Theme Party

Serves 6
Tropical Fruit Fizzle*
Jiggle 'n Giggle Sunshine Salad*
Clown Sandwich Cutouts*
Buttery Corn on a Stick*
Cookie and Cone Clowns*
*Recipe included

A circus clown is always a welcome guest at a child's birthday celebration. Ours comes in several tasty guises—Clown Sandwich Cutouts and Cookie and Cone Clowns. Usually picky eaters will be vying for seconds with these menu selections, perfect for lunchtime festivities. The foods are hearty, nutritious and easily managed by small, unsteady hands. Most important when serving youngsters with non-adventuresome appetites, these choices are familiar and popular.

No problem creating a "big top" party atmosphere. Greet little guests with a welcoming clown face on the front door and mark each chair with a personalized helium balloon tied to the back. While youngsters are seated at the table waiting to be served, have colored paper and washable markers available for them to create their own take-home clown masterpieces. Maybe your favorite sitter would be willing to dress as a clown and help lead a few games after lunch or assist with face-painting. (Clown faces, of course.)

Terrific party favor ideas include clown hand puppets, boxes of animal crackers, the inscribed balloons and ringmaster whistles.

Preparation Timetable

Day Before Party

Refrigerate all ingredients for *Tropical Fruit Fizzle* • Prepare *Jiggle 'n Giggle Sunshine Salad;* cover and refrigerate • Prepare *Cookie and Cone Clowns;* cover loosely and freeze.

Day of Party

Several Hours Before: Prepare egg salad spread and peanut butter spread for *Clown Sandwich Cutouts;* cover each and refrigerate.

Shortly Before Serving: Unmold salads onto lettuce-lined plates • Assemble sandwiches; refrigerate until serving time • Prepare *Buttery Corn on a Stick* • Prepare beverage.

Tropical Fruit Fizzle

1 (46-ounce) can (5¾ cups) fruit punch drink, chilled
3 cups orange juice, chilled
3½ cups club soda, chilled

In 3-quart nonmetal container, combine all ingredients; mix well. Serve immediately. Garnish as desired.
12 (1-cup) servings.

NUTRITION INFORMATION PER SERVING
SERVING SIZE: 1 CUP

			PERCENT U.S. RDA PER SERVING
Calories	80	Protein	*
Protein	0 g	Vitamin A	*
Carbohydrate	21 g	Vitamin C	130%
Fat	0 g	Thiamine	4%
Cholesterol	0 mg	Riboflavin	*
Sodium	20 mg	Niacin	*
Potassium	135 mg	Calcium	*
		Iron	*

*Contains less than 2% of the U.S. RDA of this nutrient.

Jiggle 'n Giggle Sunshine Salad

1 (3-ounce) package lime or lemon-flavored gelatin
1 cup boiling water
½ cup cold water
1 (8¼-ounce) can crushed pineapple, undrained
½ cup shredded carrot
Lettuce leaves

Lightly oil six ½-cup salad molds. In small bowl, dissolve gelatin in boiling water; stir in cold water and pineapple. Cover; refrigerate mixture until partially thickened, about 30 to 45 minutes. Fold in shredded carrot. Pour mixture into oiled molds. Refrigerate until firm.

To unmold, dip molds just to rim in warm water for about 10 seconds; shake slightly to loosen. Invert mold onto lettuce-lined salad plates; remove mold. If desired, top with mayonnaise or whipped cream.
6 servings.

NUTRITION INFORMATION PER SERVING
SERVING SIZE: ⅙ OF RECIPE

			PERCENT U.S. RDA PER SERVING
Calories	90	Protein	2%
Protein	2 g	Vitamin A	50%
Carbohydrate	20 g	Vitamin C	6%
Fat	0 g	Thiamine	2%
Cholesterol	0 mg	Riboflavin	*
Sodium	50 mg	Niacin	*
Potassium	125 mg	Calcium	*
		Iron	*

*Contains less than 2% of the U.S. RDA of this nutrient.

Buttery Corn on a Stick

6 ears frozen corn on the cob
6 wooden sticks
2 tablespoons margarine or butter, melted

Cook corn as directed on package. Insert sticks. Roll in melted margarine. Serve immediately.
6 servings.

NUTRITION INFORMATION PER SERVING
SERVING SIZE: ⅙ OF RECIPE

			PERCENT U.S. RDA PER SERVING
Calories	110	Protein	2%
Protein	2 g	Vitamin A	6%
Carbohydrate	16 g	Vitamin C	6%
Fat	4 g	Thiamine	4%
Cholesterol	0 mg	Riboflavin	6%
Sodium	55 mg	Niacin	6%
Potassium	180 mg	Calcium	*
		Iron	*

*Contains less than 2% of the U.S. RDA of this nutrient.

Cookie and Cone Clowns

1 (20-ounce) package refrigerated sliceable chocolate chip cookie dough
3 cups any flavor ice cream
6 sugar cones or cone cups
Assorted candies
String licorice
Frosting, tinted desired color
Decorating bag and tips

Freeze cookie dough 1 hour or longer. Heat oven to 350° F. Slice six ½-inch-thick slices from frozen cookie dough. (Prepare remaining cookie dough as directed on package.) Place slices 2 inches apart on ungreased cookie sheet. Bake at 350° F. for 10 to 13 minutes or until golden brown. Cool 2 minutes; remove from cookie sheet. Cool completely.

To assemble clowns, using ½-cup ice cream scoop, place 1 rounded scoop of ice cream in center of each cookie; press down lightly to secure. Place cone, wide end down, on top of ice cream; arrange to form hat. Freeze until firm. Remove from freezer; press candies into ice cream to form eyes and nose and licorice to form mouth. Use tinted frosting, decorating bag and star tip to make collar around ice cream and decorate cone hat. Freeze until firm.
6 servings.

NUTRITION INFORMATION PER SERVING
SERVING SIZE: ⅙ OF RECIPE

			PERCENT U.S. RDA PER SERVING
Calories	370	Protein	8%
Protein	5 g	Vitamin A	6%
Carbohydrate	54 g	Vitamin C	*
Fat	15 g	Thiamine	6%
Cholesterol	37 mg	Riboflavin	15%
Sodium	190 mg	Niacin	2%
Potassium	190 mg	Calcium	10%
		Iron	4%

*Contains less than 2% of the U.S. RDA of this nutrient.

Clown Sandwich Cutouts

EGG SALAD SPREAD
  1 egg, hard-cooked, chopped
  1 tablespoon mayonnaise
  ½ teaspoon chopped pimiento
  ¼ teaspoon chopped chives
     Dash salt and pepper

PEANUT BUTTER SPREAD
  1 tablespoon margarine or butter, softened
  1 tablespoon peanut butter
  1 tablespoon honey

  6 slices white bread
  6 slices rye or whole wheat bread
  2 tablespoons margarine or butter, softened
  2 ounces (2 slices) American Cheese

GARNISHES
  Pickle slices, olive slices, shredded cheese,
     carrot curls or slices, mushroom slices,
     nuts or green or red bell pepper strips

In small bowl, combine egg salad spread ingredients; stir until well blended. In another small bowl, combine peanut butter spread ingredients; stir until smooth and creamy.

Using 3-inch cookie cutter, cut circles from each bread slice; spread with margarine. Using 6 bread circles, spread 2 with egg salad spread, 2 with peanut butter spread and top 2 with cheese. Top with remaining bread circles to form sandwiches. Make clown face with desired garnishes.*
6 sandwiches.

TIP: *Garnishes can be secured to sandwich with cheese spread, peanut butter or mayonnaise.

NUTRITION INFORMATION PER SERVING

SERVING SIZE: 1 SANDWICH		PERCENT U.S. RDA PER SERVING	
Calories	290	Protein	10%
Protein	9 g	Vitamin A	8%
Carbohydrate	31 g	Vitamin C	*
Fat	14 g	Thiamine	10%
Cholesterol	47 mg	Riboflavin	10%
Sodium	560 mg	Niacin	10%
Potassium	120 mg	Calcium	10%
		Iron	8%

*Contains less than 2% of the U.S. RDA of this nutrient.

Pictured clockwise from upper left: Watermelon-Grape Star Salads, page 66; Orange Frosty, page 66; Peanut Butter Honey Buns, page 66

Teddy Bear Picnic Party

Serves 8
Orange Frosty*
Watermelon-Grape Star Salads*
Peanut Butter Honey Buns*
Teddy Bear Cake*
or
Big Heart Bears*
*Recipe included

No one will be shy about coming to the party, because their favorite bear will be invited too. After all, what would a Teddy Bear Picnic be without Winnie-the-Pooh and other favorite storybook bears sharing the occasion?

Half the fun of a party is anticipation and preparation. Invite the birthday boy or girl to help select or make teddy bear invitations with a note for guests to bring a favorite teddy bear companion. Then drop them in the mail or deliver them personally to the guests. Talk over ideas for party favors and decorations and shop together for the groceries you will need. Your child will love being involved right from the beginning.

You can make this a real in-the-park picnic or set up a table on your patio or under a shady tree. If the backyard is your choice and the weather is right, set up wading pools (yours or borrowed) so the children can cool off before feasting on this kid-pleasing menu. With plastic boats and other suitable toys in the pools, there should be no need for games. If you select a park setting, choose one with play equipment suited to the ages of your guests.

Since children are always amused by foods in animal shapes, you know this special cake or the Big Heart Bears will be a hit. The rest of the menu is colorful, vitamin-packed and easily eaten. A lunch or suppertime party is a better alternative than midafternoon ice cream and cake where youngsters eat little more than sweets and can spoil their appetites for a nutritious meal later.

Preparation Timetable

Day of Party

Early in the Day Prepare *Teddy Bear Cake* or *Big Heart Bears;* cover loosely and store at room temperature.

Several Hours Before: Prepare *Watermelon-Grape Star Salads;* cover and refrigerate.

Shortly Before Serving: Prepare *Peanut Butter Honey Buns* and *Orange Frosty.*

Orange Frosty

2 cups orange juice
2 envelopes whipped topping mix
2 cups crushed ice

In blender container or food processor, combine
all ingredients. Cover; blend at medium speed
until frothy, about 45 seconds. Serve immediately.
If desired, garnish with orange slice.
9 (½-cup) servings.

NUTRITION INFORMATION PER SERVING

SERVING SIZE: ½ CUP		PERCENT U.S. RDA PER SERVING	
Calories	80	Protein	*
Protein	1 g	Vitamin A	2%
Carbohydrate	11 g	Vitamin C	35%
Fat	4 g	Thiamine	2%
Cholesterol	0 mg	Riboflavin	*
Sodium	10 mg	Niacin	*
Potassium	120 mg	Calcium	*
		Iron	*

*Contains less than 2% of the U.S. RDA of this nutrient.

Watermelon-Grape Star Salads

2 (1-inch-thick) slices watermelon
1½ pounds seedless grapes, separated into
   clusters

Cut each watermelon slice into 5 wedges. On 2
serving plates, arrange 5 wedges on each plate to
form a large star. Arrange grapes around
watermelon.
10 servings.

NUTRITION INFORMATION PER SERVING

SERVING SIZE: ⅒ OF RECIPE		PERCENT U.S. RDA PER SERVING	
Calories	90	Protein	*
Protein	1 g	Vitamin A	8%
Carbohydrate	19 g	Vitamin C	30%
Fat	1 g	Thiamine	8%
Cholesterol	0 mg	Riboflavin	2%
Sodium	0 mg	Niacin	*
Potassium	240 mg	Calcium	*
		Iron	*

*Contains less than 2% of the U.S. RDA of this nutrient.

Peanut Butter Honey Buns

8 tablespoons peanut butter
8 hot dog buns, split
2 to 3 bananas, sliced
2 tablespoons honey
8 teaspoons shelled sunflower seeds, if desired

Spread 1 tablespoon peanut butter on bottom half
of each bun. Top each with banana slices; drizzle
with honey. Sprinkle 1 teaspoon sunflower seeds
on each sandwich. Replace top half of bun. Serve
immediately.
8 buns.

NUTRITION INFORMATION PER SERVING

SERVING SIZE: 1 BUN		PERCENT U.S. RDA PER SERVING	
Calories	300	Protein	10%
Protein	8 g	Vitamin A	*
Carbohydrate	40 g	Vitamin C	6%
Fat	12 g	Thiamine	15%
Cholesterol	2 mg	Riboflavin	10%
Sodium	280 mg	Niacin	20%
Potassium	360 mg	Calcium	4%
		Iron	8%

*Contains less than 2% of the U.S. RDA of this nutrient.

Big Heart Bears

CHOCOLATE PORTION
¼ cup margarine or butter
1 (10-ounce) package marshmallows
2 ounces (2 squares) semi-sweet chocolate, cut
   into pieces
6 cups crisp rice cereal

PEPPERMINT PORTION
¼ cup margarine or butter
1 (10-ounce) package marshmallows
   Red food color
½ cup crushed peppermint candy
6 cups crisp rice cereal

Line 15 × 10 × 1-inch baking pan with foil. To
prepare chocolate portion, melt margarine in
large saucepan over medium heat. Add
marshmallows and chocolate, stirring until
completely melted. Remove from heat; stir in
cereal until well coated. With wet fingers, press
mixture evenly in foil-lined pan; refrigerate until
firm. Remove from pan by lifting foil.

Line same 15 × 10 × 1-inch pan with foil. To
prepare peppermint portion, melt margarine in
large saucepan over medium heat. Add
marshmallows and 2 to 3 drops food color,
stirring until completely melted. Remove from
heat; stir in peppermint candy and cereal until
well coated. With wet fingers, press mixture
evenly in foil-lined pan; refrigerate until firm.

Using 5-inch bear-shaped or gingerbread man
cookie cutter, cut shapes from each pan of cereal
mixture. Using 1-inch heart-shaped canapé cutter,
cut hearts from center of each bear shape.
Exchange hearts between bears so each bear will
have opposite-flavor heart.
16 bears.

NUTRITION INFORMATION PER SERVING

SERVING SIZE: 1 BEAR		PERCENT U.S. RDA PER SERVING	
Calories	290	Protein	2%
Protein	2 g	Vitamin A	25%
Carbohydrate	54 g	Vitamin C	10%
Fat	7 g	Thiamine	20%
Cholesterol	0 mg	Riboflavin	20%
Sodium	330 mg	Niacin	20%
Potassium	40 mg	Calcium	*
		Iron	10%

*Contains less than 2% of the U.S. RDA of this nutrient.

Teddy Bear Cake

Teddy Bear Cake

1 package pudding-included devil's food cake mix
1¼ cups water
½ cup oil
3 eggs
1 can ready-to-spread vanilla frosting
    Chocolate sprinkles
    String licorice
    Large gumdrops
    Decorating bag and tips, if desired

Heat oven to 350° F. Grease 13 × 9-inch pan; line with waxed paper and grease again. In large bowl, combine cake mix, water, oil and eggs at low speed until moistened; beat 2 minutes at high speed. Pour batter into greased and lined pan. Bake at 350° F. for 30 to 40 minutes or until toothpick inserted in center comes out clean. Cool 10 minutes; carefully remove cake from pan. Remove waxed paper from cake; cool completely.

Cover 15 × 11-inch heavy cardboard with foil. If necessary, trim cake to obtain straight sides and level top. Center cake on foil-covered cardboard.

If desired, reserve about ⅓ cup frosting for decorating; frost sides and top of cake with remaining frosting. Using 5-inch bear-shaped cookie cutter, mark outline of 3 bear shapes on cake. Fill in bears with chocolate sprinkles; press lightly into frosting. Use string licorice and gumdrops to create balloon decorations.* Add details using gumdrops, reserved frosting, decorating bag and tips.
12 servings.

TIP: *To make balloons, sprinkle waxed paper or foil with granulated sugar. Roll or press out gumdrops to form flat, round balloons.

HIGH ALTITUDE—Above 3500 Feet: Add ¼ cup flour to dry cake mix and increase water to 1⅓ cups. Bake as directed above.

NUTRITION INFORMATION PER SERVING

SERVING SIZE: ¹/₁₂ OF RECIPE		PERCENT U.S. RDA PER SERVING	
Calories	470	Protein	6%
Protein	4 g	Vitamin A	*
Carbohydrate	66 g	Vitamin C	*
Fat	21 g	Thiamine	6%
Cholesterol	53 mg	Riboflavin	6%
Sodium	420 mg	Niacin	4%
Potassium	190 mg	Calcium	10%
		Iron	6%

*Contains less than 2% of the U.S. RDA of this nutrient.

Pictured top to bottom: Peanut Butter Nog, page 70; Mini Mouse Party Cupcakes, page 71

Mini Mouse Birthday Party

Serves 8
Peanut Butter Nog*
Orange-Yogurt Fruit Salad*
Chicken Dippers with Sauces*
Mini Mouse Party Cupcakes*
*Recipe included

*E*xpect squeals of delight from pint-sized party-goers over the big-eared, long-whiskered Mini Mouse Party Cupcakes. They are just one of the treats in store with this menu which is a refreshing change from the usual kiddie fare.

When the children arrive full of energy and excitement, engage them in a "find-the-mouse" contest. Prepare by attaching mouse faces made from paper bags or construction paper to outdoor bushes with clothespins or use wooden stakes to tuck them in hiding places. A prize goes to the one finding the most by the end of the allotted time. After a few more simple games like pin-the-tail-on-the-mouse, settle them down with a lively mouse story told from a big picture book they can all see.

When it's time to eat, mouse place cards will mark each spot. Serve colorful straws with the Peanut Butter Nog, using small, squat glasses instead of taller ones which easily tip. The calcium and protein-packed drink, along with the Orange-Yogurt Fruit Salad and Chicken Dippers, provide a hearty, fun-to-eat meal capped with the delightful cupcakes.

Preparation Timetable

Day of Party

Early in the Day: Prepare cupcakes and ice cream topping for *Mini Mouse Party Cupcakes.* Cover cupcakes loosely and store at room temperature; place decorated ice cream balls in freezer • Prepare sauces for *Chicken Dippers with Sauces;* cover each and refrigerate.

Several Hours Before Prepare *Orange-Yogurt Fruit Salad,* omitting bananas; cover and refrigerate.

Shortly Before Serving: Prepare *Chicken Dippers;* reheat sauces • Add bananas to salad • Prepare *Peanut Butter Nog* • When ready to serve dessert, top each cupcake with decorated ice cream balls.

Pictured top to bottom: Orange-Yogurt Fruit Salad; Chicken Dippers with Sauces, page 71

Peanut Butter Nog

3 cups milk
1 cup vanilla ice cream, softened
¾ cup creamy peanut butter
1 (3½-ounce) package instant vanilla pudding
    and pie filling mix

In blender container, combine all ingredients.
Cover; blend at medium-low speed until smooth
and thick, about 30 to 45 seconds. Pour into
glasses; serve immediately.
8 (½-cup) servings.

NUTRITION INFORMATION PER SERVING

SERVING SIZE: ½ CUP		PERCENT U.S. RDA PER SERVING	
Calories	280	Protein	15%
Protein	10 g	Vitamin A	4%
Carbohydrate	25 g	Vitamin C	*
Fat	16 g	Thiamine	4%
Cholesterol	14 mg	Riboflavin	10%
Sodium	230 mg	Niacin	15%
Potassium	360 mg	Calcium	15%
		Iron	4%

*Contains less than 2% of the U.S. RDA of this nutrient.

Orange-Yogurt Fruit Salad

1 (20-ounce) can pineapple chunks, drained
1 (16-ounce) can mandarin orange segments,
    drained
1 cup miniature marshmallows
4 ounces (½ cup) orange-flavored or pineapple-
    flavored yogurt
2 bananas, sliced

In medium bowl, combine pineapple, orange
segments, marshmallows and yogurt. Cover;
refrigerate several hours to blend flavors. Just
before serving, add bananas; toss to coat.
8 (½-cup) servings.

NUTRITION INFORMATION PER SERVING

SERVING SIZE: ½ CUP		PERCENT U.S. RDA PER SERVING	
Calories	120	Protein	2%
Protein	2 g	Vitamin A	8%
Carbohydrate	27 g	Vitamin C	45%
Fat	1 g	Thiamine	8%
Cholesterol	1 mg	Riboflavin	4%
Sodium	10 mg	Niacin	2%
Potassium	290 mg	Calcium	2%
		Iron	2%

Chicken Dippers with Sauces

2 (12-ounce) packages boneless breaded
    chicken pieces*

SWEET AND SOUR SAUCE
  ¼ cup firmly packed brown sugar
  1 tablespoon cornstarch
  ⅔ cup apple or pineapple juice
  ¼ cup cider vinegar
  2 tablespoons orange juice

TANGY CHILI SAUCE
  1 (8-ounce) can jellied cranberry sauce
  ⅔ cup chili sauce

Bake chicken pieces as directed on package.
Meanwhile, in small saucepan combine all
ingredients for sweet and sour sauce; mix well.
Cook over medium heat until mixture boils and
thickens, stirring constantly.

To prepare tangy chili sauce, combine ingredients
in small saucepan. Cook over low heat, stirring
mixture until well blended and thoroughly
heated. Serve hot chicken pieces with warm
sauces.** Garnish as desired.
8 servings.

MICROWAVE DIRECTIONS: To prepare sweet
and sour sauce, combine all ingredients in 2-cup
microwave-safe measuring cup. Microwave on
HIGH for 3 to 3½ minutes or until mixture
comes to a boil, stirring once halfway through
cooking; continue to microwave on HIGH an
additional 1 minute.

To prepare tangy chili sauce, combine ingredients
in 2-cup microwave-safe measuring cup.
Microwave on HIGH for 1½ to 2 minutes or until
hot, stirring once halfway through cooking.

TIPS: *The number of chicken pieces per 12-
ounce package varies among brands. Read label
information and purchase the brand that best
suits your needs.

**To serve each kid's favorite in fast-food style,
purchase small paper favor cups and fill them
with a serving of each sauce.

NUTRITION INFORMATION PER SERVING

SERVING SIZE: ⅛ OF RECIPE		PERCENT U.S. RDA PER SERVING	
Calories	360	Protein	25%
Protein	16 g	Vitamin A	8%
Carbohydrate	39 g	Vitamin C	8%
Fat	16 g	Thiamine	10%
Cholesterol	49 mg	Riboflavin	8%
Sodium	720 mg	Niacin	30%
Potassium	160 mg	Calcium	2%
		Iron	8%

Mini Mouse Party Cupcakes

1 package pudding-included devil's food cake
    mix
1¼ cups water
 ½ cup oil
 3 eggs
 1 quart (4 cups) vanilla ice cream
16 chocolate sandwich cookies or mints
    Small candies
    String licorice

Heat oven to 350° F. Line 24 muffin cups with
paper baking cups. In large bowl, combine cake
mix, water, oil and eggs at low speed until
moistened; beat 2 minutes at high speed. Fill
lined muffin cups ⅔ full. Bake at 350° F. for 20 to
30 minutes or until cupcakes spring back when
touched lightly in center. Remove from pans; cool
completely. Remove paper baking cups from 8
cupcakes; set aside. (Wrap and freeze remaining
cupcakes for later use as desired.)

Line 15 × 10 × 1-inch baking pan with waxed
paper. Using ½-cup ice cream scoop, place 8
rounded scoops of ice cream about 2 inches apart
on paper-lined pan. Decorate each scoop of ice
cream to resemble a mouse, using 2 cookies for
ears and small candies and licorice for facial
features and whiskers. Freeze until serving time.
To serve, place cupcakes in 8 serving bowls; top
each with decorated ice cream.
8 servings.

HIGH ALTITUDE—Above 3500 Feet: Add ¼
cup flour to dry cake mix and increase water to
1⅓ cups. Fill cups half full. Bake as directed
above.

NUTRITION INFORMATION PER SERVING

SERVING SIZE: ⅛ OF RECIPE		PERCENT U.S. RDA PER SERVING	
Calories	390	Protein	8%
Protein	5 g	Vitamin A	6%
Carbohydrate	51 g	Vitamin C	*
Fat	19 g	Thiamine	6%
Cholesterol	64 mg	Riboflavin	15%
Sodium	330 mg	Niacin	4%
Potassium	230 mg	Calcium	15%
		Iron	6%

*Contains less than 2% of the U.S. RDA of this nutrient.

Party-a-Saurus Cake, pages 76–77

Dinosaur Birthday Party

Serves 8
Dinosaur Punch*
Confetti Fruit Salad*
or
Kids' Favorite Fruit Salad*
Saurus Claw Sandwiches*
Party-a-Saurus Cake*
*Recipe included

---

*E*lementary school children already intrigued with prehistoric creatures through classroom study will appreciate this creative theme. Set the stage for this trip to the past with bright green dinosaur invitations traced and cut from a pattern, lettered and mailed by the birthday child.

The inviting menu is a perfect prelude or postlude to an exciting trip to a local natural history museum or a home-shown video on these fascinating reptiles that once roamed the earth. Or vary games like bingo, memory or picture lotto, anagram search, etc., to suit the theme. Instead of place cards, use lumps of clay etched with each name to look like fossils. Butcher paper makes a practical and creative tablecloth. Provide washable markers and let the kids draw their own earth-stalking monsters freehand or using stencils. After the party, the "mural" can be put up in a play area as a fond reminder of a super birthday party.

No question about the centerpiece because all eyes will be on the Party-a-Saurus Cake. Don't worry if specialty cakes aren't your forte. The easy-to-follow, step-by-step instructions, made extra easy with cake mix and prepared frosting, will guide you to the exciting results.

Preparation Timetable

Day Before Party
Place lemonade and limeade concentrates in refrigerator to thaw and refrigerate carbonated beverage for *Dinosaur Punch*.

Day of Party:
Early in the Day: Prepare *Party-a-Saurus Cake;* cover loosely and store at room temperature.

Several Hours Before: Prepare *Confetti Fruit Salad* or *Kids' Favorite Fruit Salad;* cover and refrigerate • Combine concentrates, water and food coloring for punch; refrigerate.

Shortly Before Serving: Prepare *Saurus Claw Sandwiches;* keep warm • Add carbonated beverage to punch • Spoon salad into small bowls or onto lettuce-lined plates.

Dinosaur Punch

1 (6-ounce) can frozen lemonade concentrate, thawed
½ cup frozen limeade concentrate, thawed
1 cup water
   Green food color, if desired
1 (1-liter) bottle (4¼ cups) lemon-lime flavored carbonated beverage, chilled

In 4-quart nonmetal container, combine concentrates and water; blend well. Stir in a few drops food color. Refrigerate until thoroughly chilled. Just before serving, add carbonated beverage; stir gently to blend. Serve over ice.
8 (¾-cup) servings.

NUTRITION INFORMATION PER SERVING
SERVING SIZE: ¾ CUP

		PERCENT U.S. RDA PER SERVING	
Calories	140	Protein	*
Protein	0 g	Vitamin A	*
Carbohydrate	35 g	Vitamin C	10%
Fat	0 g	Thiamine	*
Cholesterol	0 mg	Riboflavin	*
Sodium	15 mg	Niacin	*
Potassium	30 mg	Calcium	*
		Iron	*

*Contains less than 2% of the U.S. RDA of this nutrient.

Kids' Favorite Fruit Salad

1 (17-ounce) can fruit cocktail, drained
1½ cups miniature marshmallows
¼ cup maraschino cherries, halved
2 medium bananas, sliced
1 medium apple, coarsely chopped
1½ cups whipped topping or sweetened whipped cream
   Lettuce leaves

In large bowl, combine all ingredients except whipped topping and lettuce, mixing lightly. Gently fold in whipped topping. Cover; refrigerate until serving time. Spoon salad onto lettuce-lined plates; garnish with additional maraschino cherries, if desired.
8 (⅔-cup) servings.

NUTRITION INFORMATION PER SERVING
SERVING SIZE: ⅔ CUP

		PERCENT U.S. RDA PER SERVING	
Calories	180	Protein	*
Protein	1 g	Vitamin A	6%
Carbohydrate	34 g	Vitamin C	8%
Fat	4 g	Thiamine	*
Cholesterol	0 mg	Riboflavin	2%
Sodium	10 mg	Niacin	2%
Potassium	210 mg	Calcium	*
		Iron	2%

*Contains less than 2% of the U.S. RDA of this nutrient.

Confetti Fruit Salad

2 cups seeded watermelon cubes
1 cup seedless green or red grapes
1 cup multicolored miniature marshmallows
1 (11-ounce) can mandarin orange segments, drained
1 (8-ounce) can pineapple chunks, drained

In medium bowl, combine all ingredients; toss gently. Cover; refrigerate until serving time.
8 (½-cup) servings.

NUTRITION INFORMATION PER SERVING
SERVING SIZE: ½ CUP

		PERCENT U.S. RDA PER SERVING	
Calories	70	Protein	*
Protein	1 g	Vitamin A	8%
Carbohydrate	17 g	Vitamin C	30%
Fat	0 g	Thiamine	6%
Cholesterol	0 mg	Riboflavin	*
Sodium	0 mg	Niacin	*
Potassium	170 mg	Calcium	*
		Iron	2%

*Contains less than 2% of the U.S. RDA of this nutrient.

Saurus Claw Sandwiches

1 (11-ounce) can refrigerated breadsticks
2 tablespoons margarine or butter, melted
8 thin 4½-inch-square slices cooked ham, cut diagonally in half
8 individually wrapped pasteurized process American cheese food slices, cut diagonally in half
16 toothpicks

Heat oven to 350° F. Unroll dough; separate at perforations to form 8 strips. Cut each strip in half crosswise, forming 16 smaller strips. Place 1 inch apart on 1 large or 2 small ungreased cookie sheets. Using scissors or snarp knife, make three 1½-inch cuts in 1 end of each strip. To form claws, spread cut sections of each strip apart.

Bake at 350° F. for 11 to 16 minutes or until golden brown.* Brush breadsticks with margarine. Remove from cookie sheet; cool completely. Wrap 1 ham triangle and 1 cheese triangle around center of each breadstick, leaving claw uncovered. Secure with toothpick; just before eating, remove toothpick.
16 sandwiches.

TIP: *If using 2 small cookie sheets, place 1 on each rack in oven; reverse position of cookie sheets halfway through baking.

NUTRITION INFORMATION PER SERVING
SERVING SIZE: 1 SANDWICH

		PERCENT U.S. RDA PER SERVING	
Calories	130	Protein	10%
Protein	6 g	Vitamin A	4%
Carbohydrate	9 g	Vitamin C	*
Fat	7 g	Thiamine	50%
Cholesterol	19 mg	Riboflavin	6%
Sodium	420 mg	Niacin	4%
Potassium	55 mg	Calcium	8%
		Iron	4%

*Contains less than 2% of the U.S. RDA of this nutrient.

Saurus Claw Sandwiches

Party-a-Saurus Cake

1 package pudding-included devil's food cake
    mix
1¼ cups water
  ½ cup oil
  3 eggs
  2 cans ready-to-spread vanilla frosting
    Green food color
    Decorating bag and tips
    Assorted candies

Heat oven to 350° F. Grease 13 × 9-inch pan; line
with waxed paper and grease again. In large
bowl, combine cake mix, water, oil and eggs at
low speed until moistened; beat 2 minutes at high
speed. Pour into greased and lined pan. Bake at
350° F. for 30 to 40 minutes or until toothpick
inserted in center comes out clean. Cool 10
minutes; carefully remove cake from pan. Remove
waxed paper from cake; cool completely.

Cut heavy cardboard into 18 × 15-inch rectangle
or large dinosaur shape; cover with foil or colored
paper. Trace pattern pieces provided for dinosaur
onto waxed paper; cut out. Follow diagram,
position waxed paper patterns on cooled cake.
Using sharp knife, carefully cut around patterns.
If desired, for ease in frosting the cake, freeze cut
pieces 1 hour before frosting. Place cake pieces
together on foil-covered cardboard to form
dinosaur. (Store leftover cake pieces in covered
container for later use as desired.)

In medium bowl, combine frosting and ⅛ to ¼
teaspoon food color; stir until well blended.
Reserve about ½ cup frosting for decorating; frost
sides and top of cake with remaining frosting.
Add additional green food color to reserved
frosting. Using decorating bag with star tip, form
dinosaur scales with dark green frosting. Using
candies or frosting, form eyes, mouth, nose and
claws.
16 servings.

HIGH ALTITUDE—Above 3500 Feet: Add ¼
cup flour to dry cake mix and increase water to
1⅓ cups. Bake as directed above.

NUTRITION INFORMATION PER SERVING
SERVING SIZE: ¹⁄₁₆ OF
RECIPE

		PERCENT U.S. RDA PER SERVING	
Calories	420	Protein	2%
Protein	2 g	Vitamin A	*
Carbohydrate	61 g	Vitamin C	*
Fat	19 g	Thiamine	2%
Cholesterol	33 mg	Riboflavin	4%
Sodium	320 mg	Niacin	2%
Potassium	130 mg	Calcium	6%
		Iron	4%

*Contains less than 2% of the U.S. RDA of this nutrient.

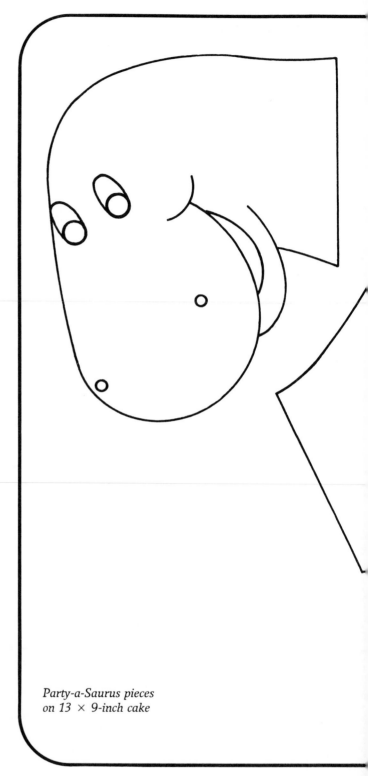

*Party-a-Saurus pieces
on 13 × 9-inch cake*

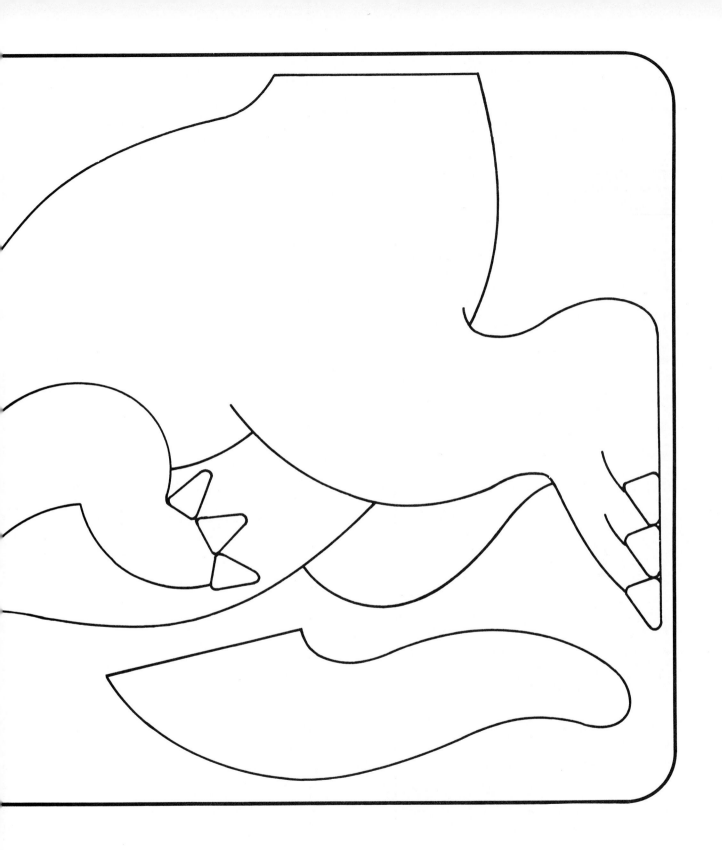

Pictured left to right: 7th Inning Hot Dogs, page 80; Baseball All-Star Cookie Treat, page 81

Baseball All-Star Birthday Party

Serves 8
Cran-Orange Refresher*
Peanuts   Popcorn
Fruity Orange Cups*
7th Inning Hot Dogs*
Baseball Lover's Sundae*
Baseball All-Star Cookie Treat*

*Recipe included

*T*he bases are loaded with lots of great food and fun for this solid hit of a party which is terrific for a birthday or a Little League get-together. If it's a birthday, rally 'round the theme with baseball-inspired invitations and decorations in favorite team colors (pennants, balloons, crepe paper, etc.). Or honor this truly American sport with a red, white and blue motif.

Instead of usual party games, treat the gang to a game at the local ball park or arrange a backyard or sandlot game with guests participating.

Sports fans will cheer this menu of all-American favorites. If the game is in the backyard, serve some of the Cran-Orange Refresher along with the peanuts and popcorn to keep energy high until the last home run. Serve the rest of the food at a picnic table or casual area of your home where the kids will feel comfortable. Sports fans will delight in the eye-catching Baseball Lover's Sundae served in a bowl set inside an adult's baseball mitt. And the Baseball All-Star Cookie Treat makes a nifty dessert alternative to cake because it's easily toted, if necessary. On another occasion, you might want to take this dessert to a game or practice to pass during the 7th inning stretch.

Preparation Timetable

Day Before Party
Refrigerate cranberry juice cocktail for *Cran-Orange Refresher.*

Day of Party
Early in the Day Prepare *Baseball All-Star Cookie Treat;* cover loosely and store at room temperature • Scoop ice cream into bowl for *Baseball Lover's Sundae;* cover and freeze.

Several Hours Before Place peanuts in small serving bowl; pop popcorn and place in serving bowl • Prepare *Fruity Orange Cups;* cover and refrigerate.

Shortly Before Serving: Prepare *7th Inning Hot Dogs;* keep warm • Prepare beverage • When ready to serve dessert, complete preparation of sundae.

Cran-Orange Refresher

4 cups cranberry juice cocktail, chilled
2 pints (4 cups) orange sherbet, softened

In blender container, combine half of cranberry juice cocktail and half of sherbet. Cover; blend until smooth. Repeat with other half of ingredients. Serve immediately.
8 (1-cup) servings.

NUTRITION INFORMATION PER SERVING

SERVING SIZE: 1 CUP		PERCENT U.S. RDA PER SERVING	
Calories	210	Protein	*
Protein	1 g	Vitamin A	*
Carbohydrate	48 g	Vitamin C	80%
Fat	2 g	Thiamine	*
Cholesterol	7 mg	Riboflavin	2%
Sodium	45 mg	Niacin	*
Potassium	120 mg	Calcium	6%
		Iron	*

*Contains less than 2% of the U.S. RDA of this nutrient.

Fruity Orange Cups

4 medium oranges
1 (8-ounce) can pineapple chunks, drained, cut into bite-sized pieces
⅔ cup miniature marshmallows
8 maraschino cherries

Cut oranges in half crosswise. With sharp knife, cut around edges of orange halves to remove entire orange from peel; set orange cups aside. Cut orange into segments, removing membrane. In medium bowl, combine orange segments, pineapple and marshmallows; stir gently to blend. Spoon fruit mixture into reserved orange cups. Top each with cherry.
8 servings.

NUTRITION INFORMATION PER SERVING

SERVING SIZE: ⅛ OF RECIPE		PERCENT U.S. RDA PER SERVING	
Calories	60	Protein	*
Protein	1 g	Vitamin A	2%
Carbohydrate	14 g	Vitamin C	60%
Fat	0 g	Thiamine	4%
Cholesterol	0 mg	Riboflavin	*
Sodium	0 mg	Niacin	*
Potassium	150 mg	Calcium	2%
		Iron	*

*Contains less than 2% of the U.S. RDA of this nutrient.

7th Inning Hot Dogs

2 (8-ounce) cans refrigerated crescent dinner rolls
8 cheese-filled or regular wieners, cut in half

Heat oven to 375° F. Separate dough into 8 rectangles; firmly press perforations to seal. Cut each rectangle in half lengthwise. Place a wiener half lengthwise on 1 end of dough strip. Fold dough in half over wiener; press short edges to seal, leaving sides open. Place on ungreased cookie sheet. Bake at 375° F. for 11 to 13 minutes or until golden brown. Serve with ketchup, mustard and pickle relish, if desired.
16 servings.

NUTRITION INFORMATION PER SERVING

SERVING SIZE: 1/16 OF RECIPE		PERCENT U.S. RDA PER SERVING	
Calories	180	Protein	6%
Protein	5 g	Vitamin A	*
Carbohydrate	12 g	Vitamin C	*
Fat	12 g	Thiamine	4%
Cholesterol	18 mg	Riboflavin	2%
Sodium	480 mg	Niacin	4%
Potassium	100 mg	Calcium	*
		Iron	4%

*Contains less than 2% of the U.S. RDA of this nutrient.

Baseball Lover's Sundae

1 quart (4 cups) chocolate chip or vanilla ice cream
½ cup chocolate fudge ice cream topping
1 cup (8 cookies) broken cream-filled peanut butter sandwich cookies

Scoop ice cream into 1-quart bowl. Freeze until firm, if desired. Drizzle fudge topping over ice cream; sprinkle with broken cookies. To serve, place bowl in adult-sized baseball glove; spoon into individual serving dishes.
8 servings.

NUTRITION INFORMATION PER SERVING

SERVING SIZE: ⅛ OF RECIPE		PERCENT U.S. RDA PER SERVING	
Calories	260	Protein	6%
Protein	4 g	Vitamin A	6%
Carbohydrate	33 g	Vitamin C	*
Fat	12 g	Thiamine	2%
Cholesterol	34 mg	Riboflavin	10%
Sodium	125 mg	Niacin	*
Potassium	190 mg	Calcium	10%
		Iron	2%

*Contains less than 2% of the U.S. RDA of this nutrient.

Baseball All-Star Cookie Treat

Baseball All-Star Cookie Treat

1 (10-ounce) package marshmallows
⅓ cup margarine or butter
6 cups crisp rice cereal
1 can ready-to-spread vanilla frosting
   Frosting, tinted desired color
   Decorating bag and tips

Grease 12-inch pizza pan.* In large saucepan over medium heat, melt marshmallows and margarine, stirring constantly until mixture is smooth. Add cereal; stir until evenly coated. Press mixture evenly into greased pan. Cool completely. Spread frosting over cereal mixture to within 1 inch of edge. Using tinted frosting, decorating bag and tips, decorate frosted area to resemble baseball. Add message, if desired. Cut into wedges to serve. **10 servings.**

MICROWAVE DIRECTIONS: Place cereal in large bowl. Place marshmallows and margarine in microwave-safe 2-quart measuring cup or bowl. Microwave on HIGH for 1 minute; stir. Microwave on HIGH for 1 to 2 minutes or until marshmallows are almost melted; stir until smooth. Pour marshmallow mixture over cereal; stir until evenly coated. Continue as directed above.

TIP: *To make cookie treat without a pizza pan, press cereal mixture into 12-inch circle on large waxed paper-lined cookie sheet.

NUTRITION INFORMATION PER SERVING

SERVING SIZE: ⅒ OF RECIPE		PERCENT U.S. RDA PER SERVING	
Calories	410	Protein	2%
Protein	2 g	Vitamin A	20%
Carbohydrate	70 g	Vitamin C	10%
Fat	14 g	Thiamine	15%
Cholesterol	0 mg	Riboflavin	15%
Sodium	380 mg	Niacin	15%
Potassium	35 mg	Calcium	*
		Iron	8%

*Contains less than 2% of the U.S. RDA of this nutrient.

Pictured left to right: Popcorn Munch Mix, page 84; Flavored Cola Fixin's, page 84

Teen Video Party

Serves 8 to 12

Flavored Cola Fixin's*   Popcorn Munch Mix*
Dilly Dip*   Assorted Cut-Up Fresh Vegetables
Taco Dip*   Tortilla or Corn Chips
Thick Pan Pizza*
Giant Ice Cream Sandwich Sundae*

*Recipe included

*T*hrowing a party for teens is no trick at all with the right ingredients—a popular activity, ample refreshments, casual, comfortable surroundings and a gathering of good friends. Mix generously and enjoy the results—a great time had by all.

A video party is a natural theme because visiting, viewing and nibbling can be easily combined with few challenges to the hosts. For invitations, write out all the particulars on mock movie theater tickets, including the name of the video under the heading of "now showing" or "sneak preview." Suggest casual dress and let guests know that supper will be served at "intermission." Arrange your "home theater" for maximum viewing with chairs and large cushions in rows or a semicircle.

Set out dips just before guests arrive so they are available for snacking during the first half of the movie. Flavored Cola Fixin's should be placed where they are easily accessible for refills throughout the evening. Pass the Popcorn Munch Mix in colorful paper bags just before the lights dim, and have seconds close by in a giant bowl with a handy help-yourself scoop. Intermission is pizza time; if hungry appetites warrant the need, make two pizzas, preparing each individually. After the movie, bring on the refreshing Giant Ice Cream Sandwich Sundae.

Preparation Timetable

Day Before Party

Refrigerate cola for *Flavored Cola Fixin's* • Prepare *Giant Ice Cream Sandwich Sundae;* cover and freeze • Prepare topping for sundae; cool, cover and refrigerate.

Day of Party

Early in the Day: Prepare *Dilly Dip* and cream cheese portion of *Taco Dip;* cover and refrigerate • Cut up assorted fresh vegetables to be served with dips; place in plastic bags and refrigerate • Prepare *Popcorn Munch Mix;* place in airtight container and store at room temperature.

Several Hours Before Remove sundae topping from refrigerator; pour into serving bowl and let stand at room temperature until serving time • About 1½ hours before serving, begin preparation of *Thick Pan Pizza.*

Shortly Before Serving: Arrange cut-up vegetables on tray or platter; place tortilla or corn chips in basket or bowl • Bake pizza • Complete preparation of taco dip • Set out all ingredients for cola fixin's on serving table • About 15 minutes before serving dessert, remove ice cream sandwich sundae from freezer. Drizzle topping over individual servings.

Flavored Cola Fixin's

LEMON COLA
¾ cup cola, chilled
Twist of lemon

CHERRY COLA
¾ cup cola, chilled
1 tablespoon grenadine syrup
1 tablespoon maraschino cherry juice

CHOCOLATE COLA
¾ cup cola, chilled
2 to 3 tablespoons chocolate syrup

VANILLA COLA
¾ cup cola, chilled
¼ teaspoon vanilla

Select desired flavor of cola. In shaker or tall glass, combine ingredients; shake or stir to blend. Add ice. Garnish as desired.
1 (¾-cup) serving.

NUTRITION INFORMATION: Variables in this recipe make it impossible to calculate nutrition information.

Popcorn Munch Mix

1 quart (4 cups) popped popcorn
1 cup bite-sized crispy wheat squares cereal
1 cup goldfish crackers
1 cup sesame cracker sticks or miniature pretzels
½ cup peanuts
¼ cup margarine or butter
¼ teaspoon seasoned salt
¼ teaspoon garlic powder
1½ teaspoons Worcestershire sauce

Heat oven to 250° F. In large bowl, combine popcorn, cereal, crackers, cracker sticks and peanuts; set aside. Melt margarine in 13 × 9-inch pan in oven. Remove from oven; stir in seasoned salt, garlic powder and Worcestershire sauce. Drizzle margarine mixture over popcorn mixture in bowl; stir to coat. Place popcorn mixture in same 13 × 9-inch pan. Bake at 250° F. for 1 hour, stirring every 15 minutes. Cool completely. Store in airtight container.
6 cups.

NUTRITION INFORMATION PER SERVING
SERVING SIZE: 1 CUP

		PERCENT U.S. RDA PER SERVING	
Calories	310		
Protein	7 g	Protein	10%
Carbohydrate	33 g	Vitamin A	6%
Fat	17 g	Vitamin C	4%
Cholesterol	0 mg	Thiamine	15%
Sodium	590 mg	Riboflavin	4%
Potassium	180 mg	Niacin	20%
		Calcium	2%
		Iron	10%

Dilly Dip

1½ cups dairy sour cream
⅔ cup mayonnaise
2 tablespoons instant minced onion
2 tablespoons parsley flakes
2 tablespoons dried dill weed
2 teaspoons celery salt
Cut-up fresh vegetables

In small bowl, combine all ingredients except fresh vegetables; mix well. Cover; refrigerate several hours to blend flavors. Serve with cut-up fresh vegetables.
2 cups.

NUTRITION INFORMATION PER SERVING
SERVING SIZE: 1 TABLESPOON DIP

		PERCENT U.S. RDA PER SERVING	
Calories	60		
Protein	0 g	Protein	*
Carbohydrate	1 g	Vitamin A	2%
Fat	6 g	Vitamin C	*
Cholesterol	8 mg	Thiamine	*
Sodium	140 mg	Riboflavin	*
Potassium	30 mg	Niacin	*
		Calcium	*
		Iron	*

*Contains less than 2% of the U.S. RDA of this nutrient.

Taco Dip

1 (8-ounce) package cream cheese, softened
1 (8-ounce) carton dairy sour cream
1 (6-ounce) package frozen avocado dip, thawed
1 teaspoon lemon juice
4 drops hot pepper sauce
2 cups torn lettuce
1 (4-ounce) can chopped ripe olives, drained
1 (4-ounce) can chopped green chiles, drained
4 green onions, sliced
1 tomato, peeled, seeded, chopped
4 ounces (1 cup) shredded Cheddar cheese
Tortilla or corn chips

In small bowl, combine cream cheese, sour cream, avocado dip, lemon juice and hot pepper sauce; blend well. Spread mixture on large serving plate. Top with lettuce, olives, chiles, onions, tomato and cheese. Serve with tortilla or corn chips.
10 to 12 servings.

TIP: Cream cheese mixture can be made several hours ahead; store in refrigerator. Just before serving, top with lettuce, olives, chiles, onions, tomato and cheese.

NUTRITION INFORMATION PER SERVING
SERVING SIZE: 1/12 OF DIP

		PERCENT U.S. RDA PER SERVING	
Calories	190		
Protein	5 g	Protein	8%
Carbohydrate	5 g	Vitamin A	30%
Fat	17 g	Vitamin C	35%
Cholesterol	39 mg	Thiamine	2%
Sodium	310 mg	Riboflavin	6%
Potassium	150 mg	Niacin	*
		Calcium	10%
		Iron	4%

*Contains less than 2% of the U.S. RDA of this nutrient.

Thick Pan Pizza

CRUST
- **1** package hot roll mix
- **½** cup grated Parmesan cheese
- **1¼** cups water heated to 120 to 130°F.
- **2** tablespoons oil

TOPPING
- **1** pound ground Italian sausage
- **¼** cup grated Parmesan cheese
- **¼** teaspoon dried oregano leaves, crushed
- **1** (8-ounce) can tomato sauce
- **1** medium onion, sliced into rings
- **1** medium green bell pepper, sliced into rings
- **8** ounces provolone cheese, sliced
- **2** ounces (½ cup) shredded Cheddar cheese

Generously grease 14-inch pizza pan or 15 × 10 × 1-inch baking pan. In large bowl, combine flour mixture with yeast from foil packet and ½ cup Parmesan cheese; mix well. Stir in *hot* water and oil until dry particles are moistened. Turn dough out onto lightly floured surface. With greased or floured hands, shape dough into a ball. Knead dough for 2 to 3 minutes until no longer sticky. With greased hands, pat dough into greased pan, forming rim around edge of pan. Generously prick with fork. Cover loosely with plastic wrap and cloth towel. Let rise on countertop for 15 minutes. Place oven rack at lowest position; heat oven to 425° F.

Meanwhile, in medium skillet brown sausage; drain. Uncover dough; top with sausage. Sprinkle with ¼ cup Parmesan cheese and oregano. Pour tomato sauce over cheese and oregano; top with onion and green pepper rings. Bake at 425° F. on lowest oven rack for 20 to 30 minutes or until crust is deep golden brown. Top with provolone cheese; sprinkle with Cheddar cheese. Bake an additional 5 to 10 minutes, or until cheese is melted. Let stand 5 minutes before serving.
8 servings.

NUTRITION INFORMATION PER SERVING
SERVING SIZE: ⅛ OF RECIPE

Calories	510	Protein	40%
Protein	25 g	Vitamin A	15%
Carbohydrate	47 g	Vitamin C	15%
Fat	24 g	Thiamine	40%
Cholesterol	55 mg	Riboflavin	30%
Sodium	1270 mg	Niacin	25%
Potassium	360 mg	Calcium	40%
		Iron	15%

Giant Ice Cream Sandwich Sundae

- **2** (15-ounce) packages fudge brownie mix
- **⅔** cup water
- **½** cup oil
- **2** eggs
- **1** (6-ounce) package (1 cup) semi-sweet chocolate chips, if desired
- **½** gallon (8 cups) any flavor ice cream, slightly softened

TOPPING
- **2** cups powdered sugar
- **⅔** cup semi-sweet chocolate chips
- **1** cup evaporated milk
- **½** cup margarine or butter
- **1** teaspoon vanilla

Heat oven to 350° F. Line two 12-inch pizza pans with foil. In large bowl, combine brownie mixes, water, oil, eggs and 1 cup chocolate chips; beat 50 strokes with spoon. Spread half of batter in each foil-lined pan. Bake at 350° F. for 15 to 20 minutes. *Do not overbake.* Cool; freeze 1 to 2 hours for ease in handling. Remove from pans; remove foil. To assemble, place 1 brownie round on serving plate. Spoon softened ice cream evenly over brownie. Top with remaining brownie. Cover; freeze until firm.

Meanwhile, in medium saucepan combine powdered sugar, ⅔ cup chocolate chips, milk and margarine. Bring to a boil; cook 8 minutes, stirring constantly. Remove from heat; stir in vanilla. Cool.

Let ice cream sandwich stand at room temperature for 10 to 15 minutes before serving. Cut into wedges; drizzle with topping.
16 servings.

HIGH ALTITUDE—Above 3500 Feet: Add 3 tablespoons flour to dry brownie mix. Bake as directed above.

NUTRITION INFORMATION PER SERVING
SERVING SIZE: ⅟₁₆ OF RECIPE

Calories	650	Protein	10%
Protein	7 g	Vitamin A	10%
Carbohydrate	85 g	Vitamin C	2%
Fat	31 g	Thiamine	4%
Cholesterol	57 mg	Riboflavin	20%
Sodium	340 mg	Niacin	4%
Potassium	380 mg	Calcium	15%
		Iron	8%

Pizza Dippers, page 88

Backyard Burger Bash

❀

Serves 12
Sodas Sparkling Water
Pizza Dippers*
Sparkling Rainbow Melon*
and/or
Pasta Vegetable Salad*
Burgers for Grilling*
Wheel-o'-Fun Cakes*

*Recipe included

When great weather and a birthday coincide, move the party outdoors for a carefree cookout. This summertime sampler, featuring fast-to-fix favorites, is tailor-made for teens. It will satisfy a dozen hearty appetites, even after a vigorous game of tennis, some roller blading or an afternoon at the beach or pool.

A great advantage of this casual feast—the chef doesn't miss out on any of the fun. The host can tend the grill while guests visit nearby, nibbling on the zesty Pizza Dippers and savoring the aroma of the burgers. For a Texas touch, brush meat patties with your favorite bottled or homemade barbecue sauce when they are in the final cooking stages. The Wheel-o'-Fun Cakes are unique. Choose from remaining ingredient ideas for color and crunch or substitute your own creative choices.

Keep decor in tune with the informal menu by using a denim table covering or runner accented with bandana-print napkins. (Napkin rings add interest and weight when the day is windy.) Have candles ready to ward off unwanted insects and keep the centerpiece simple. A bouquet of daisies or other garden flowers tucked in a pottery jug or pitcher would be ideal. Or try a spray of ribbon-wrapped dried flowers. One safety note: always situate grill in a well-ventilated area away from congestion.

Preparation Timetable

Day Before Party
Refrigerate beverages • If making *Sparkling Rainbow Melon*, place limeade concentrate in refrigerator to thaw, and refrigerate carbonated beverage.

Day of Party
Early in the Day: Prepare *Wheel-o'-Fun Cakes;* refrigerate • If making *Pasta Vegetable Salad,* prepare salad omitting tomatoes; cover and refrigerate •

Several Hours Before: Prepare melon salad omitting carbonated beverage; cover and refrigerate • Prepare and shape patties for *Burgers for Grilling;* cover and refrigerate.

Shortly Before Serving: Add tomatoes to vegetable salad and/or stir carbonated beverage into melon salad • Prepare *Pizza Dippers* • Grill burgers.

Sparkling Rainbow Melon

2 cups watermelon balls or cubes
2 cups honeydew melon balls or cubes
2 cups cantaloupe balls or cubes
⅓ cup frozen limeade concentrate, thawed
½ cup lemon-lime-flavored carbonated
    beverage, chilled

In large bowl, combine all ingredients except
carbonated beverage; blend well. Refrigerate 1 to
2 hours to blend flavors. Just before serving, add
carbonated beverage, stirring gently.
12 (½-cup) servings.

NUTRITION INFORMATION PER SERVING

SERVING SIZE: ½ CUP		PERCENT U.S. RDA PER SERVING	
Calories	50	Protein	*
Protein	1 g	Vitamin A	20%
Carbohydrate	12 g	Vitamin C	35%
Fat	0 g	Thiamine	2%
Cholesterol	0 mg	Riboflavin	*
Sodium	5 mg	Niacin	*
Potassium	190 mg	Calcium	*
		Iron	*

*Contains less than 2% of the U.S. RDA of this nutrient.

Pasta Vegetable Salad

16 ounces (4½ cups) uncooked medium shell
    macaroni
½ cup sliced zucchini
½ cup small broccoli florets
2 tablespoons sliced green onions
1 (6-ounce) can mushroom slices broiled in
    butter, undrained
1 (6-ounce) jar marinated artichoke hearts,
    drained, quartered
1 (3½-ounce) package pepperoni slices, halved
⅔ cup prepared Italian dressing
1 cup cherry tomatoes, halved

Cook macaroni to desired doneness as directed on
package. Drain; rinse with cold water.

In large bowl, combine cooked macaroni and
remaining ingredients except tomatoes; toss
gently. Cover; refrigerate at least 3 hours to
blend flavors. Just before serving, stir in tomatoes.
12 (½-cup) servings.

NUTRITION INFORMATION PER SERVING

SERVING SIZE: ½ CUP		PERCENT U.S. RDA PER SERVING	
Calories	260	Protein	10%
Protein	8 g	Vitamin A	4%
Carbohydrate	32 g	Vitamin C	10%
Fat	11 g	Thiamine	30%
Cholesterol	7 mg	Riboflavin	10%
Sodium	370 mg	Niacin	20%
Potassium	200 mg	Calcium	*
		Iron	10%

*Contains less than 2% of the U.S. RDA of this nutrient.

Pizza Dippers

1 (10-ounce) can refrigerated pizza crust
2 tablespoons margarine or butter, melted
1 teaspoon dried basil leaves
½ teaspoon dried oregano leaves
4 ounces (1 cup) shredded mozzarella cheese
1 (8-ounce) can prepared pizza sauce, heated

Heat oven to 350° F. Grease 1 large or 2 small
cookie sheets. Unroll dough; cut rectangle in half
crosswise forming two 6½ × 8-inch pieces. Cut
each piece into eight 1-inch strips. Place strips 1
inch apart on greased cookie sheet. Brush each
with margarine; sprinkle evenly with basil and
oregano leaves.

Bake at 350° F. for 11 to 17 minutes or until
golden brown. Remove from oven; sprinkle strips
with cheese. Bake an additional 1 to 2 minutes or
until cheese is melted. Serve immediately with
heated pizza sauce as dip.
16 servings.

NUTRITION INFORMATION PER SERVING

SERVING SIZE: ¹⁄₁₆ OF RECIPE		PERCENT U.S. RDA PER SERVING	
Calories	90	Protein	6%
Protein	4 g	Vitamin A	4%
Carbohydrate	10 g	Vitamin C	*
Fat	3 g	Thiamine	4%
Cholesterol	4 mg	Riboflavin	4%
Sodium	220 mg	Niacin	4%
Potassium	20 mg	Calcium	6%
		Iron	4%

*Contains less than 2% of the U.S. RDA of this nutrient.

Burgers for Grilling

3 pounds lean ground beef
⅔ cup dry bread crumbs
⅓ cup finely chopped onion
¾ teaspoon garlic salt
½ teaspoon pepper
1 tablespoon Worcestershire sauce
2 eggs
12 hamburger buns

In medium bowl, combine all ingredients except
hamburger buns; blend well. Shape mixture into
12 patties. Place patties on grill about 4 inches
from medium coals. Cook until browned on both
sides and of desired doneness. Serve on buns with
favorite toppings.
12 servings.

NUTRITION INFORMATION PER SERVING

SERVING SIZE: ¹⁄₁₂ OF RECIPE		PERCENT U.S. RDA PER SERVING	
Calories	370	Protein	40%
Protein	25 g	Vitamin A	*
Carbohydrate	26 g	Vitamin C	*
Fat	18 g	Thiamine	15%
Cholesterol	108 mg	Riboflavin	20%
Sodium	450 mg	Niacin	30%
Potassium	310 mg	Calcium	4%
		Iron	20%

*Contains less than 2% of the U.S. RDA of this nutrient.

Wheel-o'-Fun Cakes

Wheel-o'-Fun Cakes

**1 package pudding-included devil's food cake
    mix**
1¼ cups water
½ cup oil
3 eggs
**2 (8-ounce) containers (6 cups) frozen whipped
    topping, thawed**
    **Any one or a combination of small candies,
    assorted nuts and cookies, cut into pieces**

Heat oven to 350° F. Grease and flour two 8- or
9-inch round cake pans. In large bowl, combine
cake mix, water, oil and eggs at low speed until
moistened; beat 2 minutes at high speed. Pour
batter into greased and floured pans. Bake at
350° F. for 25 to 35 minutes or until toothpick
inserted in center comes out clean. Cool 15
minutes; remove from pans. Cool completely.

Place each cake on serving plate; frost sides and
tops with whipped topping. Score each cake into
6 equal wedges. Top each wedge with 2
tablespoons desired topping. Refrigerate until
serving time.
12 servings.

HIGH ALTITUDE—Above 3500 Feet: Add ¼
cup flour to dry cake mix and increase water to
1⅓ cups. Bake as directed above.

NUTRITION INFORMATION PER SERVING
SERVING SIZE: ¹/₁₂ OF RECIPE

		PERCENT U.S. RDA PER SERVING	
Calories	480	Protein	8%
Protein	5 g	Vitamin A	8%
Carbohydrate	53 g	Vitamin C	*
Fat	28 g	Thiamine	8%
Cholesterol	60 mg	Riboflavin	8%
Sodium	430 mg	Niacin	6%
Potassium	190 mg	Calcium	10%
		Iron	8%

*Contains less than 2% of the U.S. RDA of this nutrient.

Pictured clockwise from top left: Parmesan-Garlic Bubble Loaf, page 92; Citrus Salad Toss, page 92; Turkey with Apple-Cran Sauce, pages 92–93

Benchmark Birthday Party

Serves 8 to 10
Citrus Salad Toss*
Parmesan-Garlic Bubble Loaf*
Turkey with Apple-Cran Sauce*
Buttered Green Beans
Celebration Cake*
Coffee   Tea
*Recipe included

Celebrating a terrific thirtieth, fabulous fortieth, nifty fiftieth, sensational sixtieth or on up? Each birthday calls for a VIP (Very Important Party) for a VIP (Very Important Person) to be honored. Even the most reluctant celebrant is certain to enjoy our sit-down dinner menu for eight to ten close friends.

Admittedly a bit more sophisticated than the other menus in this section, it still retains the pleasure of favorite foods dressed for party presentation. The Parmesan-Garlic Bubble Loaf, prepared ahead but reheated for irresistible warm-from-the-oven flavor and aroma, plus the colorfully garnished turkey breast complete the inviting main course. The Celebration Cake is as festive as they come, and so attractive it can serve as the centerpiece if you choose. It's as versatile as your imagination allows. Decorate with a bright yellow star or a colorful bouquet of fresh fruits, as pictured on page 2, to suit the tastes and style of the honored guest.

Personalize the party by beginning with invitations featuring a picture of the birthday person or a drawing depicting a well-known hobby or special interest. If guests are bringing gifts, request that they relate to a particular theme or hobby. Ideas? Lures for the weekend fisherman, kitchen utensils for the gourmet cook, best sellers for the avid reader or gardening supplies for the green-thumber.

Preparation Timetable

Several Days Ahead

Prepare *Parmesan-Garlic Bubble Loaf;* cool completely, wrap in foil and freeze.

Day Before Party

Wash lettuce and prepare topping and dressing for *Citrus Salad Toss;* refrigerate lettuce and dressing and store topping at room temperature • Bake *Celebration Cake* but do not fill or frost; cool completely, place on foil-covered cardboard, cover and refrigerate.

Day of Party

Early in the Day: Remove bubble loaf from freezer to thaw • Combine lettuce, onion and oranges for salad; refrigerate • Fill, frost and decorate cake.

Several Hours Before: Prepare *Turkey with Apple-Cran Sauce.*

Shortly Before Serving: Warm foil-wrapped bubble loaf in oven with turkey • Prepare green beans • If necessary, reheat apple-cran sauce • Prepare coffee and/or tea • Slice avocado; complete preparation of salad.

Citrus Salad Toss

TOPPING
⅓ cup whole pecans
2 tablespoons sugar

SALAD
4 cups torn leaf lettuce
4 cups torn romaine lettuce
½ red onion, thinly sliced
2 oranges, peeled, sectioned
1 ripe avocado, peeled, thinly sliced

DRESSING
⅓ cup oil
2 tablespoons lime juice
1 tablespoon sugar
1 tablespoon orange juice
½ teaspoon grated lime peel
½ teaspoon grated orange peel

In small skillet, combine pecans and 2 tablespoons sugar; cook over low heat until sugar is melted and pecans are coated, stirring constantly. Immediately spread on foil or greased cookie sheet. Cool; break apart. Set aside.

In large salad bowl, combine all salad ingredients except avocado; toss gently. Refrigerate until thoroughly chilled.

In jar with tight-fitting lid, combine all dressing ingredients; shake until well blended and sugar is dissolved. Just before serving, add avocado to salad; pour dressing over chilled salad and toss gently. Sprinkle with pecans.
8 to 10 servings.

NUTRITION INFORMATION PER SERVING
SERVING SIZE: 1/10 OF RECIPE

		PERCENT U.S. RDA PER SERVING	
Calories	330	Protein	4%
Protein	3 g	Vitamin A	40%
Carbohydrate	22 g	Vitamin C	80%
Fat	26 g	Thiamine	10%
Cholesterol	0 mg	Riboflavin	8%
Sodium	10 mg	Niacin	6%
Potassium	640 mg	Calcium	6%
		Iron	6%

Parmesan-Garlic Bubble Loaf

1 package hot roll mix
1 cup water heated to 120 to 130° F.
2 tablespoons margarine or butter, softened
1 egg
¼ cup margarine or butter, melted
2 tablespoons grated Parmesan cheese
4 teaspoons sesame seed
½ teaspoon garlic powder

Generously grease 12-cup fluted tube pan. In large bowl, combine yeast from foil packet with

flour mixture; blend well. Stir in *hot* water, 2 tablespoons margarine and egg until dough pulls away from sides of bowl. Turn dough out onto lightly floured surface. With greased or floured hands, shape dough into a ball. Knead dough 5 minutes until smooth. Cover with large bowl; let rest 5 minutes.

Divide dough into 32 pieces. Place half of dough pieces in greased pan. Drizzle with 2 tablespoons melted margarine; sprinkle with 1 tablespoon cheese, 2 teaspoons sesame seed and ¼ teaspoon garlic powder. Repeat with remaining dough pieces, margarine, cheese, sesame seed and garlic powder. Cover loosely with plastic wrap and cloth towel. Let rise in warm place (80 to 85° F.) 30 minutes.

Heat oven to 375° F. Uncover dough. Bake at 375° F. for 20 to 25 minutes or until deep golden brown. Immediately invert onto serving plate.
16 to 20 servings.

TIP: To reheat, wrap loosely in foil; heat at 350° F. for 15 to 20 minutes.

HIGH ALTITUDE—Above 3500 Feet: No change.

NUTRITION INFORMATION PER SERVING
SERVING SIZE: 1/20 OF RECIPE

		PERCENT U.S. RDA PER SERVING	
Calories	120	Protein	4%
Protein	3 g	Vitamin A	2%
Carbohydrate	17 g	Vitamin C	*
Fat	4 g	Thiamine	10%
Cholesterol	11 mg	Riboflavin	8%
Sodium	210 mg	Niacin	6%
Potassium	40 mg	Calcium	*
		Iron	4%

*Contains less than 2% of the U.S. RDA of this nutrient.

Turkey with Apple-Cran Sauce

2 tablespoons oil
¼ teaspoon onion powder
⅛ teaspoon garlic powder
1 (4 to 5-pound) fresh or frozen whole turkey breast, thawed
1 teaspoon dried thyme leaves
Salt and pepper

APPLE-CRAN SAUCE
1 medium (1 cup) red apple, coarsely chopped
2 teaspoons margarine or butter
2 tablespoons cornstarch
1½ cups cranberry-apple drink
½ cup whole berry cranberry sauce

Heat oven to 350° F. In small bowl, combine oil, onion powder and garlic powder; brush turkey breast on all sides with oil mixture. Rub thyme over all sides of turkey; sprinkle with salt and pepper. Place turkey, skin side up, on rack in roasting pan. Bake at 350° F. for 2½ to 3 hours or until internal temperature reaches 170° F. and turkey is tender throughout. Let turkey stand 15 minutes before slicing.

Meanwhile, in small skillet cook apple in margarine; set aside. Place cornstarch in small saucepan; add cranberry-apple drink, blending well. Stir in cranberry sauce. Cook over medium heat until mixture boils and thickens, stirring constantly. Add apple; stir until thoroughly heated. Serve sauce with sliced turkey.

8 to 10 servings.

NUTRITION INFORMATION PER SERVING
SERVING SIZE: ⅒ OF RECIPE

		PERCENT U.S. RDA PER SERVING	
Calories	280	Protein	70%
Protein	42 g	Vitamin A	*
Carbohydrate	16 g	Vitamin C	15%
Fat	5 g	Thiamine	4%
Cholesterol	117 mg	Riboflavin	10%
Sodium	115 mg	Niacin	50%
Potassium	440 mg	Calcium	2%
		Iron	15%

*Contains less than 2% of the U.S. RDA of this nutrient.

Celebration Cake

CAKE
1 package pudding-included lemon or yellow cake mix
1 (3-ounce) package cream cheese, softened
1 cup water
3 eggs
2 teaspoons grated lemon peel

PINEAPPLE FILLING
½ cup sugar
3 tablespoons cornstarch
1 (8-ounce) can crushed pineapple in heavy syrup, drained, reserving liquid
¼ cup lemon juice
2 tablespoons margarine or butter

FROSTING
¾ cup margarine or butter, softened
¾ cup shortening
1½ teaspoons vanilla
5 cups powdered sugar
3 to 5 tablespoons half-and-half or milk

Yellow decorating sugar
Yellow food coloring
Decorating bag and tips

Heat oven to 350° F. Grease 13 × 9-inch pan; line with waxed paper and grease again. In large bowl, combine all cake ingredients at low speed until moistened; beat 2 minutes at high speed.

Pour batter into greased and lined pan. Bake at 350° F. for 30 to 40 minutes or until toothpick inserted in center comes out clean. Cool 10 minutes; carefully remove cake from pan. Remove waxed paper from cake; cool completely.

In medium saucepan, combine sugar and cornstarch. Add water to reserved pineapple liquid to equal 1 cup. Add liquid, pineapple, lemon juice and 2 tablespoons margarine to sugar mixture; blend well. Cook over medium heat until mixture boils and thickens, stirring constantly. Remove from heat; cool.

In large bowl, combine ¾ cup margarine, shortening and vanilla. Gradually add powdered sugar, beating at medium speed until creamy. Add half-and-half; beat at high speed until light and fluffy, adding additional half-and-half if necessary for desired spreading consistency.

Cover 15 × 11-inch heavy cardboard with foil. Using toothpicks as a cutting guideline and a long-bladed sharp knife, slice cake in half horizontally. Center 1 cake layer on foil-covered cardboard. Spread with filling. Place second cake layer over filling. Reserve ¾ to 1 cup frosting for decorating; frost sides and top of cake with remaining frosting. Use 4-inch star-shaped cookie cutter or prepare star stencil using waxed paper. Place cookie cutter or stencil on cake and sprinkle yellow sugar to fill in star. Tint half of reserved frosting with several drops food coloring. With decorating bag and tips, outline star shape and pipe decorative border and birthday message on cake using reserved white and yellow frosting.

20 servings.

FRESH FRUIT VARIATION: Prepare lemon cake as directed above. Fill and frost cake; omit star pattern decoration. Garnish by using fresh strawberries, lemon slices and mint leaves to form flowers as shown on page 2.

TIP: To obtain 2 layers without slicing cake, cake can be baked in two 13 × 9-inch pans. Prepare pans as directed above. Pour half of batter into each pan. Baking time will be 10 minutes less than above.

HIGH ALTITUDE—Above 3500 Feet: Add ⅓ cup flour to dry cake mix. Bake as directed above.

NUTRITION INFORMATION PER SERVING
SERVING SIZE: 1/20 OF RECIPE

		PERCENT U.S. RDA PER SERVING	
Calories	410	Protein	4%
Protein	3 g	Vitamin A	8%
Carbohydrate	54 g	Vitamin C	2%
Fat	20 g	Thiamine	4%
Cholesterol	38 mg	Riboflavin	6%
Sodium	270 mg	Niacin	2%
Potassium	50 mg	Calcium	4%
		Iron	2%

Pictured left to right on front plate: Cashew-Rice Pilaf, page 104; Petite Rack of Lamb, page 105; Dilly Peas and Mushrooms, page 104

Holiday Celebrations

Every month of the year we can look forward to one or more official holidays or special dates to celebrate. What perfect occasions for sharing our time and talents and opening our homes to family and friends! With a theme already announced by the calendar, special menus and trimmings—whether traditional or innovative—can bring each holiday to life in a very personal way.

Holidays are often busy times for everyone, and the following menu sugestions, together with their Preparation Timetables, are designed to assist and streamline your holiday hosting. And since holidays are also a time to welcome countless friends and relatives, many of the recipes are ideally suited to entertaining large groups. There are many make-aheads to eliminate last-minute chaos, and the uncomplicated but creative garnishes make each dish worthy of the festive date it honors.

These recipes can easily be used as parts of a puzzle. Mix and match them with traditional family favorites and put them together for other festive holidays like Easter, St. Patrick's Day, Halloween or Twelfth Night. Every menu calls out, "Let's celebrate!"

Glittery Gift Cake, page 101

Holiday Open House

Serves 12
Party Punch*
Mini-Wreath Sandwiches*
Decked-Out Egg Halves*   Star Bites*
Snack Beef 'n Bread*
Vegetable Crudités with Nacho Cheese Sauce*
Creamy Spinach Dip*
Glittery Gift Cake*
Coffee   Tea
*Recipe included

---

*F*estive foods and conviviality are two favorite features of the holiday season. Put them together, and what do you have? An open house like this one with an irresistible array of marvelous munchies and wonderful ways to meet and greet old friends and new.

As a host, plan to mingle with your guests because this roster of recipes includes many make-ahead options with only a few last-minute touches. Highlighted are light, refreshing and nutritious selections, a welcome change from the usual calorie-laden canapés and sweets found on many buffets. Fresh vegetables, high-protein ingredients and other healthful treats will provide a pleasant surprise for weight-conscious party goers.

Recipes such as Star Bites and Mini-Wreath Sandwiches use common ingredients yet add interesting flair to a buffet table, and their simplicity allows you to trim precious minutes from preparation time. Be sure to check out the suggestions for buffet presentation, page 15, so guests can serve themselves with ease.

"Taking the cake" as a sensational centerpiece is the Glittery Gift Cake. It is so spectacular, you may want to make two—one to cut and serve as guests come and go and the other to remain as a showpiece to be savored later with your family. By the way, this gem requires only four main ingredients, and a cake mix can be used if desired. But that's your secret as you reap the raves.

Preparation Timetable

Day Before Open House

Refrigerate catawba grape juice and carbonated beverage for *Party Punch;* prepare ice ring for punch and freeze • Wash and cut up *Vegetable Crudités;* place in plastic bags and refrigerate • Prepare *Glittery Gift Cake,* omitting edible glitter; cover loosely and store at room temperature.

Day of Open House

Early in the Day: Prepare *Mini-Wreath Sandwiches, Decked-Out Egg Halves, Star Bites, Snack Beef 'n Bread* and *Creamy Spinach Dip;* cover and refrigerate.

Shortly Before Serving: Prepare *Nacho Cheese Sauce;* keep warm over low heat • Arrange cut-up vegetables on platter • Garnish appetizers • Prepare punch; garnish bowl with ice ring • Sprinkle edible glitter on cake • Prepare coffee and/or tea.

Party Punch

1 (6-ounce) can frozen lemonade concentrate,
    thawed
1 (6-ounce) can frozen orange juice
    concentrate, thawed
2 cups white catawba grape juice, chilled
1 (1-liter) bottle (4¼ cups) lemon-lime-flavored
    carbonated beverage, chilled
    Ice ring or ice mold, if desired

In punch bowl, combine lemonade and orange
juice concentrates. Just before serving, add grape
juice and carbonated beverage; stir gently to
blend. Garnish punch bowl with ice ring.
15 (½-cup) servings.

NUTRITION INFORMATION PER SERVING
SERVING SIZE: ½ CUP

		PERCENT U.S. RDA PER SERVING	
Calories	100	Protein	*
Protein	1 g	Vitamin A	*
Carbohydrate	25 g	Vitamin C	35%
Fat	0 g	Thiamine	2%
Cholesterol	0 mg	Riboflavin	2%
Sodium	10 mg	Niacin	*
Potassium	150 mg	Calcium	*
		Iron	*

*Contains less than 2% of the U.S. RDA of this nutrient.

Star Bites

2 medium zucchini or cucumbers
½ cup olive-and-pimiento cream cheese spread

Cut each zucchini into 2-inch-long pieces; make
five V-shaped cuts about ½ inch deep lengthwise
around outside of each piece. Remove zucchini
from cuts. Cut crosswise into ¼-inch-thick slices
to form star shapes. Or cut zucchini into ¼-inch-
thick slices; using 1½-inch star-shaped canapé
cutter, cut stars from each slice. Pipe or spoon
about ½ teaspoon cream cheese spread on center
of each slice. Refrigerate until serving time.
Garnish as desired.
About 44 appetizers.

NUTRITION INFORMATION PER SERVING
SERVING SIZE: 1 APPETIZER

		PERCENT U.S. RDA PER SERVING	
Calories	12	Protein	*
Protein	0 g	Vitamin A	*
Carbohydrate	1 g	Vitamin C	2%
Fat	1 g	Thiamine	*
Cholesterol	3 mg	Riboflavin	*
Sodium	15 mg	Niacin	*
Potassium	45 mg	Calcium	*
		Iron	*

*Contains less than 2% of the U.S. RDA of this nutrient.

Decked-Out Egg Halves

½ cup mayonnaise
¼ teaspoon onion powder
¼ teaspoon dried dill weed
 8 eggs, hard-cooked, cut in half lengthwise
16 small cooked shrimp

In small bowl, combine mayonnaise, onion
powder and dill weed; mix well. Place egg halves,
cut side up, on serving tray. Spoon ½ to 1
teaspoon mayonnaise mixture onto each egg. Top
each with shrimp. Garnish as desired. If
necessary, cover and refrigerate until serving
time.
16 appetizers.

NUTRITION INFORMATION PER SERVING
SERVING SIZE: 1 APPETIZER

		PERCENT U.S. RDA PER SERVING	
Calories	90	Protein	4%
Protein	4 g	Vitamin A	2%
Carbohydrate	1 g	Vitamin C	*
Fat	8 g	Thiamine	*
Cholesterol	110 mg	Riboflavin	8%
Sodium	75 mg	Niacin	*
Potassium	40 mg	Calcium	*
		Iron	*

*Contains less than 2% of the U.S. RDA of this nutrient.

Snack Beef 'n Bread

¼ cup butter or margarine, softened
½ cup dairy sour cream
2 teaspoons prepared mustard
¼ teaspoon garlic powder
   Dash dried dill weed
1 (11-ounce) can refrigerated French loaf,
   baked, cooled
6 ounces cooked roast beef, thinly sliced

In small bowl, beat butter until smooth. Add sour
cream, mustard, garlic powder and dill weed;
blend well. Slice bread into sixteen ¾-inch slices;
spread each with about 1 teaspoon sour cream
mixture. Top with roast beef slices; spoon or pipe
about ½ teaspoon sour cream mixture on top of
beef. Garnish as desired. If necessary, cover and
refrigerate until serving time.
16 appetizers.

NUTRITION INFORMATION PER SERVING
SERVING SIZE: 1 APPETIZER

		PERCENT U.S. RDA PER SERVING	
Calories	110	Protein	8%
Protein	6 g	Vitamin A	2%
Carbohydrate	9 g	Vitamin C	*
Fat	6 g	Thiamine	6%
Cholesterol	21 mg	Riboflavin	4%
Sodium	140 mg	Niacin	6%
Potassium	60 mg	Calcium	*
		Iron	6%

*Contains less than 2% of the U.S. RDA of this nutrient.

Pictured clockwise from left: Star Bites, page 98; Decked-Out Egg Halves, page 98; Mini-Wreath Sandwiches

Mini-Wreath Sandwiches

1 (5-ounce) jar sharp Cheddar cheese food
    spread
1 (3-ounce) package cream cheese, softened
1 tablespoon chopped onion
⅛ teaspoon garlic powder
10 slices white or whole wheat bread
1 cup chopped fresh parsley, dill weed or
    watercress
    Sliced pimiento

In food processor bowl with metal blade or
blender container, combine cheese food spread,
cream cheese, onion and garlic powder; process
until smooth. Using 2-inch round cookie,
doughnut or biscuit cutter, cut rounds from bread
slices. Spread cheese mixture onto rounds. Press
parsley around edges to form wreath. Garnish
with pimiento. Refrigerate until serving time.
30 appetizers.

NUTRITION INFORMATION PER SERVING
SERVING SIZE: 1
APPETIZER

		PERCENT U.S. RDA PER SERVING	
Calories	50	Protein	2%
Protein	2 g	Vitamin A	4%
Carbohydrate	5 g	Vitamin C	4%
Fat	2 g	Thiamine	2%
Cholesterol	6 mg	Riboflavin	2%
Sodium	120 mg	Niacin	*
Potassium	35 mg	Calcium	4%
		Iron	2%

*Contains less than 2% of the U.S. RDA of this nutrient.

Vegetable Crudités with Nacho Cheese Sauce, page 101

Vegetable Crudités with Nacho Cheese Sauce

1 16-ounce package pasteurized process cheese
  spread with mild jalapeño chiles, cubed
6 cups assorted vegetables such as:
  Broccoli or cauliflower florets
  Red, green or yellow bell pepper strips
  Celery sticks
  Carrot sticks
  Jicama sticks

Melt cheese-spread cubes in small saucepan over
low heat, stirring until smooth. Pour into fondue
pot or bowl; keep warm. Arrange vegetables on
platter; serve immediately with warm cheese dip.
12 servings.

MICROWAVE DIRECTIONS: Place cheese-
spread cubes in 4-cup microwave-safe measuring
cup. Microwave on HIGH for 3 to 4 minutes or
until melted, stirring once halfway through
cooking.

NUTRITION INFORMATION: Variables in this
recipe make it impossible to calculate nutrition
information.

Creamy Spinach Dip

  1 (8-ounce) carton dairy sour cream
  1 cup mayonnaise
  ½ teaspoon celery salt
  ½ teaspoon dried dill weed
  ¼ teaspoon onion salt
  ¼ cup chopped green onions
  1 (10-ounce) package frozen chopped spinach
    in a pouch, thawed, well drained
  1 (8-ounce) can water chestnuts, drained,
    finely chopped
  3 tablespoons chopped pimiento or red bell
    pepper, if desired

In medium bowl, combine sour cream,
mayonnaise, celery salt, dill weed and onion salt.
Stir in green onions, spinach, water chestnuts and
pimiento. Cover; refrigerate several hours to
blend flavors.
3½ cups.

NUTRITION INFORMATION PER SERVING
SERVING SIZE: 1   PERCENT U.S. RDA PER
TABLESPOON   SERVING

Calories	40	Protein	*
Protein	0 g	Vitamin A	2%
Carbohydrate	1 g	Vitamin C	2%
Fat	4 g	Thiamine	*
Cholesterol	4 mg	Riboflavin	*
Sodium	60 mg	Niacin	*
Potassium	50 mg	Calcium	*
		Iron	*

*Contains less than 2% of the U.S. RDA of this nutrient.

Glittery Gift Cake

1 (13 × 9-inch) baked cake (use your favorite
  recipe or mix)
1 can ready-to-spread vanilla frosting
6 ounces (1 cup) vanilla milk chips or 6 ounces
  vanilla candy coating
¼ cup light corn syrup
  Green food color
  Red food color
  Edible glitter*

Grease 13 × 9-inch pan; line with waxed paper
and grease again. Prepare and bake cake as
directed in recipe or according to package
directions. Cool slightly; carefully remove cake
from pan. Remove waxed paper from cake; cool
completely. Invert cake onto large tray or foil-
covered cardboard. Frost sides and top of cake
with vanilla frosting.

To prepare ribbons and bow, in small saucepan
combine vanilla milk chips and corn syrup. Melt
over low heat until mixture is smooth, stirring
constantly. Refrigerate 15 to 20 minutes or until
mixture is firm enough to knead. Knead until
smooth. Divide mixture into 2 parts, making ¼
and ¾ portions. Knead a few drops green food
color into ¼ portion. Wrap in plastic wrap.
Knead a few drops red food color into ¾ portion.
Place red mixture between 2 sheets of parchment
paper or on surface sprinkled lightly with
powdered sugar; roll out mixture into 16 × 6-inch
rectangle.** With knife or pastry wheel, cut
lengthwise into eight strips ¾ inch wide. Place
strips on cake to resemble ribbon on a package;
fold additional strips to form bow.

To cut out holly leaves, roll out green mixture as
directed above to about ⅛-inch thickness. Cut out
8 leaves using holly leaf cookie cutter; score veins
with tip of knife. Tuck leaves around bow for
garnish. Sprinkle ribbon and leaves with edible
glitter. (See p. 96.)
12 servings.

TIPS: *Edible glitter is available at kitchen
specialty shops.

**To keep parchment paper from slipping while
rolling out ribbons, tape to counter.

NUTRITION INFORMATION: Variables in this
recipe make it impossible to calculate nutrition
information.

Strawberry Heart Tart, page 105

Valentine's Day Celebration Dinner

Serves 2
Chilled Champagne
Spinach-Citrus Salad*
Sesame Rounds*
Petite Rack of Lamb*   Mint Jelly
Cashew-Rice Pilaf*   Dilly Peas and Mushrooms*
Strawberry Heart Tart*
Coffee   Tea
*Recipe included

Valentine's Day seems a most appropriate time to celebrate—an engagement, an anniversary perhaps, or simply the joy of spending an intimate evening with someone dear.

Our gourmet menu begins with chilled champagne, the beverage most often associated with special occasions. The enticing entree, Petite Rack of Lamb, is as elegant as it is easy to prepare. Cashew Rice Pilaf, Dilly Peas and Mushrooms and your choice of crunchy herb breads bring marvelous texture and flavor to this impressive fare. (See photo page 94.) Follow the timetable suggestions for steps that can be completed well in advance of serving time.

The deluxe desserts are in a class by themselves, so whichever one you choose will be dramatic and delicious. Both feature make-ahead steps; however, to avoid a soggy crust in the Strawberry Heart Tart, assemble the tart close to serving time as the timetable suggests.

Provide an exceptional setting for this splendid repast to add to the lovely memories—beautiful background music, flickering candles and your finest tableware on lovely linens. Another romantic accent—a dainty centerpiece of sweetheart roses and baby's breath.

Preparation Timetable

Day Before Dinner

Refrigerate champagne • Clean spinach for *Spinach-Citrus Salad;* place in plastic bag and refrigerate.

Day of Dinner

Early in the Day: Toast sesame seed and prepare orange mixture for salad; cover and refrigerate • Gather and measure out ingredients for *Cashew-Rice Pilaf* • Spoon mint jelly into serving dish; cover and refrigerate.

Several Hours Before: Prepare crust for *Strawberry Heart Tart;* cool completely, cover loosely and store at room temperature.

An Hour Before: Prepare *Petite Rack of Lamb* • Complete preparation of tart.

Shortly Before Serving: Prepare pilaf • Prepare *Sesame Rounds* • Complete preparation of salad • Prepare *Dilly Peas and Mushrooms* • Prepare coffee and/or tea.

Spinach-Citrus Salad

2 small oranges, peeled, sectioned (¾ cup)*
1 slice sweet red onion, separated into rings
2 tablespoons red wine vinegar
½ teaspoon sesame seed, toasted**
1½ cups torn fresh spinach

In shallow bowl, combine oranges and onion. Add red wine vinegar; mix gently. Sprinkle with sesame seed. Cover; refrigerate at least 2 hours to blend flavors, stirring occasionally. Just before serving, place spinach in small bowl. Add orange mixture; toss to combine.
2 servings.

TIPS: *To section oranges, peel down to membrane. With sharp knife, cut and remove orange sections; discard membrane.

**To toast sesame seed, spread on cookie sheet. Bake at 375° F. for about 5 minutes or until light golden brown, stirring occasionally. Do *not* microwave.

NUTRITION INFORMATION PER SERVING
SERVING SIZE: ½ OF RECIPE

		PERCENT U.S. RDA PER SERVING	
Calories	80	Protein	4%
Protein	3 g	Vitamin A	60%
Carbohydrate	15 g	Vitamin C	110%
Fat	1 g	Thiamine	8%
Cholesterol	0 mg	Riboflavin	6%
Sodium	35 mg	Niacin	2%
Potassium	450 mg	Calcium	8%
		Iron	6%

Cashew-Rice Pilaf

2 tablespoons margarine or butter
2 to 3 tablespoons finely chopped onion
½ cup uncooked regular rice
1 cup chicken broth
¼ teaspoon salt
¼ cup cashews, coarsely chopped
2 tablespoons chopped fresh parsley

Melt margarine in medium saucepan. Cook onion in margarine until tender. Add rice; stir until coated with margarine. Stir in chicken broth and salt. Cover; simmer 25 to 30 minutes or until rice is tender and liquid is absorbed. Stir in cashews and parsley.
2 to 3 servings.

NUTRITION INFORMATION PER SERVING
SERVING SIZE: ⅓ OF RECIPE

		PERCENT U.S. RDA PER SERVING	
Calories	270	Protein	8%
Protein	6 g	Vitamin A	8%
Carbohydrate	30 g	Vitamin C	2%
Fat	14 g	Thiamine	15%
Cholesterol	0 mg	Riboflavin	4%
Sodium	520 mg	Niacin	10%
Potassium	210 mg	Calcium	2%
		Iron	10%

Sesame Rounds

1 (11-ounce) can refrigerated breadsticks
1 teaspoon water
1 teaspoon Dijon mustard
1 egg
4 teaspoons sesame seed

Heat oven to 425° F. Grease 2 cookie sheets. Separate but do not unroll breadsticks. Place coils 4 inches apart on greased cookie sheets. Press each coil to 5-inch circle; pinch to seal separations. Prick entire surface with fork. In small bowl, beat water, mustard and egg until well blended. Brush over circles of dough. Generously sprinkle with sesame seed. Bake at 425° F. for 7 to 10 minutes or until golden brown on edges. Serve warm.
8 rolls.

NUTRITION INFORMATION PER SERVING
SERVING SIZE: 1 ROLL

		PERCENT U.S. RDA PER SERVING	
Calories	120	Protein	6%
Protein	4 g	Vitamin A	*
Carbohydrate	17 g	Vitamin C	*
Fat	4 g	Thiamine	100%
Cholesterol	27 mg	Riboflavin	8%
Sodium	260 mg	Niacin	6%
Potassium	35 mg	Calcium	*
		Iron	6%

*Contains less than 2% of the U.S. RDA of this nutrient.

Dilly Peas and Mushrooms

1 cup frozen sweet peas
½ cup sliced fresh mushrooms
½ cup water
¼ cup dairy sour cream
⅛ to ¼ teaspoon dried dill weed
⅛ teaspoon salt
Dash pepper

In small skillet, combine peas, mushrooms and water. Cover; bring to a boil. Cook over medium-high heat about 3 minutes or until vegetables are crisp-tender; drain. Stir in remaining ingredients.
2 (½-cup) servings.

MICROWAVE INSTRUCTIONS: In 1-quart microwave-safe casserole, combine peas, mushrooms and *2 tablespoons* water; cover tightly. Microwave on HIGH for 3 to 4 minutes or until vegetables are crisp-tender, stirring once halfway through cooking; drain. Stir in remaining ingredients.

NUTRITION INFORMATION PER SERVING
SERVING SIZE: ½ CUP

		PERCENT U.S. RDA PER SERVING	
Calories	120	Protein	8%
Protein	5 g	Vitamin A	15%
Carbohydrate	12 g	Vitamin C	15%
Fat	7 g	Thiamine	15%
Cholesterol	13 mg	Riboflavin	10%
Sodium	230 mg	Niacin	10%
Potassium	220 mg	Calcium	4%
		Iron	8%

Petite Rack of Lamb

1 (6-rib) rack of lamb (about ¾ pound)
1 tablespoon chopped fresh parsley
½ teaspoon dried rosemary leaves
¼ teaspoon salt
¼ teaspoon dry mustard
¼ teaspoon pepper
1 tablespoon margarine or butter, softened
1 small garlic clove, minced

MEAT SAUCE
¼ cup beef broth
¼ cup dry white wine*
1 to 2 teaspoons cornstarch
1 tablespoon water

Heat oven to 450° F. Place lamb in shallow roasting pan with rib bones pointing down. In small bowl, combine parsley, rosemary, salt, dry mustard, pepper, margarine and garlic; mix well. Rub mixture on lamb. Insert meat thermometer in thickest part of meat.

Roast at 450° F. for about 30 minutes or until meat thermometer reaches 140° F. (rare) or 160° F. (medium). Place lamb on platter; keep warm.

If meat sauce is desired, drain fat from meat drippings. Add beef broth to pan; stir to loosen brown particles. Strain into small saucepan; add wine. In small bowl, combine cornstarch and water; stir into wine mixture. Bring to a boil, stirring constantly until clear and thickened. Serve sauce with meat.

2 servings.

TIP: *One-fourth cup additional beef broth can be substituted for the dry white wine.

NUTRITION INFORMATION PER SERVING
SERVING SIZE: ½ OF RECIPE

		PERCENT U.S. RDA PER SERVING	
Calories	270	Protein	30%
Protein	21 g	Vitamin A	6%
Carbohydrate	4 g	Vitamin C	2%
Fat	16 g	Thiamine	4%
Cholesterol	65 mg	Riboflavin	10%
Sodium	540 mg	Niacin	25%
Potassium	320 mg	Calcium	2%
		Iron	10%

Strawberry Heart Tart

1 (15-ounce) package refrigerated pie crusts
1 teaspoon flour
3 tablespoons red currant jelly
1 teaspoon orange-flavored liqueur or orange juice
1 (8-ounce) package cream cheese, softened
¼ cup powdered sugar
1 tablespoon orange-flavored liqueur or orange juice
3 to 4 cups strawberries, cut in half

Heat oven to 450° F. Allow 1 crust pouch to stand at room temperature for 15 to 20 minutes. (Refrigerate remaining crust for later use as desired). Unfold pie crust; peel off top plastic sheet. Press out fold lines; sprinkle flour over crust. Turn crust, flour side down, onto ungreased cookie sheet; peel off remaining plastic sheet. Using paper pattern as guide, cut crust in heart shape.* Fold edges in ½ inch and flute. Generously prick crust with fork. Bake at 450° F. for 9 to 11 minutes or until golden brown. Cool.

In small saucepan, heat jelly with 1 teaspoon liqueur until melted; brush a thin layer over crust. In small bowl, combine cream cheese, powdered sugar and 1 tablespoon liqueur; beat until smooth. Spread over crust. Arrange strawberry halves, cut side down and slightly overlapping, on cream cheese mixture. Brush with remaining jelly mixture. Refrigerate until serving time.

8 to 10 servings.

TIPS: *To make pattern for 1 large tart, cut a piece of paper into a heart shape about 10½ inches high. To make pattern for 4 mini-tarts, cut a piece of paper into a heart shape about 4½ inches high. Continue as directed above.

Small heart garnishes can be cut from remaining pie crust; sprinkle with sugar and bake with heart tart(s).

NUTRITION INFORMATION PER SERVING
SERVING SIZE: ⅟₁₀ OF RECIPE

		PERCENT U.S. RDA PER SERVING	
Calories	230	Protein	4%
Protein	3 g	Vitamin A	6%
Carbohydrate	24 g	Vitamin C	80%
Fat	14 g	Thiamine	*
Cholesterol	30 mg	Riboflavin	6%
Sodium	150 mg	Niacin	*
Potassium	180 mg	Calcium	2%
		Iron	4%

*Contains less than 2% of the U.S. RDA of this nutrient.

Pictured clockwise from left: M's for Mom, page 109; Easy Cheesy Blender Soufflé, page 108; Melon Wedges, page 108

Mother's Day Brunch

Serves 4
Grapefruit Juice Cocktail*
Melon Wedges*
M's for Mom*
Easy Cheesy Blender Soufflé*
Maple-Glazed Canadian Bacon*
Sherbet 'n Angelcake*
Coffee   Tea
*Recipe included

Certainly a sentimental favorite as holidays go, Mother's Day has been observed as a national event since the early 1900s. The idea for the annual observance is thought to have roots in England where "Mothering Sunday" has been devoutly observed for many generations. Today we appreciate the opportunity to laud mothers on this second Sunday in May with special family festivities.

Begin Mother's Day with a cheery "Good morning" and breakfast in bed. While the guest of honor relaxes, the rest of the family can join in the simple steps to this tasty tribute.

Actually, preparation begins the day before when the dessert, using only two purchased ingredients, is assembled and secreted in the freezer. Keep the whimsical "M" bread shapes warm while baking the blender soufflé, or briefly reheat them in the microwave just before serving. The Canadian bacon is speedily heated in skillet or microwave just before serving as well. If melon is not at its seasonal best, substitute berries or another colorful fruit. Any will be congenial with the zesty yogurt dressing.

A final note—cleanup is the cook's job, so treat Mom to a sparkling kitchen as well as this super-special breakfast.

Preparation Timetable

Day Before Brunch

Refrigerate grapefruit juice and carbonated beverage for *Grapefruit Juice Cocktail* • Prepare *Sherbet 'n Angelcake;* cover and freeze.

Morning of Brunch

Prepare *M's for Mom;* keep warm • Prepare *Easy Cheesy Blender Soufflé* • While soufflé is baking, prepare *Melon Wedges* • Prepare *Maple-Glazed Canadian Bacon;* keep warm over very low heat or reheat in microwave just before serving • Prepare juice cocktail • Prepare coffee and/or tea.

Grapefruit Juice Cocktail

2 cups pink grapefruit juice cocktail, chilled
2 cups lemon-lime-flavored carbonated
    beverage, chilled
    Crushed ice

In 1-quart nonmetal pitcher, combine grapefruit juice cocktail and lemon-lime carbonated beverage; blend well. Fill glasses with crushed ice. Pour juice over ice. Serve immediately.
4 (1-cup) servings.

NUTRITION INFORMATION PER SERVING
SERVING SIZE: 1 CUP

		PERCENT U.S. RDA PER SERVING	
Calories	100	Protein	*
Protein	1 g	Vitamin A	*
Carbohydrate	25 g	Vitamin C	70%
Fat	0 g	Thiamine	2%
Cholesterol	0 mg	Riboflavin	*
Sodium	15 mg	Niacin	*
Potassium	170 mg	Calcium	*
		Iron	*

*Contains less than 2% of the U.S. RDA of this nutrient.

Easy Cheesy Blender Soufflé

2 tablespoons grated Parmesan cheese
4 eggs
4 ounces (1 cup) shredded Cheddar cheese
1 (3-ounce) package cream cheese, softened
⅓ cup milk
¼ cup grated Parmesan cheese
½ teaspoon dry mustard
1 tablespoon chopped fresh chives
1 tablespoon chopped fresh parsley

Heat oven to 350° F. Butter four 10-ounce custard cups or soufflé dishes; sprinkle bottom and sides of cups with 2 tablespoons Parmesan cheese. Place cups on cookie sheet or in 13 × 9-inch pan. In blender container, combine eggs, Cheddar cheese, cream cheese, milk, ¼ cup Parmesan cheese and dry mustard; cover. Blend for 30 seconds or until smooth and well blended. Stir in chives and parsley. Carefully pour into buttered and coated custard cups. Bake at 350° F. for 25 to 30 minutes or until puffy, set and light golden brown. Serve immediately.
4 servings.

NUTRITION INFORMATION PER SERVING
SERVING SIZE: ¼ OF RECIPE

		PERCENT U.S. RDA PER SERVING	
Calories	320	Protein	30%
Protein	20 g	Vitamin A	20%
Carbohydrate	3 g	Vitamin C	*
Fat	25 g	Thiamine	2%
Cholesterol	274 mg	Riboflavin	25%
Sodium	490 mg	Niacin	*
Potassium	160 mg	Calcium	40%
		Iron	6%

*Contains less than 2% of the U.S. RDA of this nutrient.

Melon Wedges

1 (8-ounce) carton vanilla yogurt
1 to 2 tablespoons frozen orange juice
    concentrate, thawed
1 cantaloupe, seeded, cut into quarters or
    slices
1 kiwifruit, peeled, sliced
    Nutmeg

In small bowl, combine yogurt and orange juice concentrate; blend well. Place cantaloupe wedges on individual serving plates. Spoon 2 tablespoons yogurt mixture over each wedge. Top with kiwifruit. Sprinkle with nutmeg. Serve immediately. Pass any remaining yogurt mixture.
4 servings.

NUTRITION INFORMATION PER SERVING
SERVING SIZE: ¼ OF RECIPE

		PERCENT U.S. RDA PER SERVING	
Calories	120	Protein	6%
Protein	4 g	Vitamin A	90%
Carbohydrate	25 g	Vitamin C	140%
Fat	1 g	Thiamine	6%
Cholesterol	3 mg	Riboflavin	8%
Sodium	50 mg	Niacin	4%
Potassium	660 mg	Calcium	10%
		Iron	2%

Maple-Glazed Canadian Bacon

1 (8-ounce) package Canadian bacon
1 tablespoon margarine or butter
½ cup maple-flavored syrup
¾ teaspoon cinnamon

Cut bacon into 8 equal slices about ¼ inch thick. Melt margarine in large skillet; stir in syrup and cinnamon. Place bacon slices in syrup mixture; turn to coat slices with sauce. Arrange in single layer, slightly overlapping. Simmer over medium heat 5 minutes or until bacon is thoroughly heated. Place bacon slices on serving platter. Pour sauce into small bowl or pitcher; serve with bacon.
4 servings.

NUTRITION INFORMATION PER SERVING
SERVING SIZE: ¼ OF RECIPE

		PERCENT U.S. RDA PER SERVING	
Calories	220	Protein	20%
Protein	12 g	Vitamin A	2%
Carbohydrate	27 g	Vitamin C	15%
Fat	7 g	Thiamine	30%
Cholesterol	28 mg	Riboflavin	6%
Sodium	830 mg	Niacin	20%
Potassium	210 mg	Calcium	*
		Iron	2%

*Contains less than 2% of the U.S. RDA of this nutrient.

Sherbet 'n Angelcake

M's for Mom

1 (11-ounce) can refrigerated breadsticks
1 tablespoon margarine or butter, melted
1 tablespoon sugar
½ teaspoon cinnamon

Heat oven to 350° F. Unroll dough; separate at
perforations to form 8 strips. Form each strip of
dough into an M shape on 1 large or 2 small
ungreased cookie sheets. (Use flat side of strip for
top of M.) Brush with margarine. In small bowl,
combine sugar and cinnamon; blend well.
Sprinkle mixture evenly over M-shaped strips.
Bake at 350° F. for 12 to 17 minutes or until
golden brown. Immediately remove from cookie
sheets. Serve warm.

8 servings.

NUTRITION INFORMATION PER SERVING

SERVING SIZE: ⅛ OF RECIPE		PERCENT U.S. RDA PER SERVING	
Calories	120	Protein	4%
Protein	3 g	Vitamin A	*
Carbohydrate	18 g	Vitamin C	*
Fat	4 g	Thiamine	100%
Cholesterol	0 mg	Riboflavin	6%
Sodium	250 mg	Niacin	6%
Potassium	25 mg	Calcium	*
		Iron	6%

*Contains less than 2% of the U.S. RDA of this nutrient.

Sherbet 'n Angelcake

1 loaf angel food or sponge cake
(approximately 12 × 5 inches)
1 quart (4 cups) any flavor sherbet

Slice cake in half horizontally to form 2 layers.
Place 1 layer on serving tray; spread evenly with
about 2 cups of the sherbet. Top with remaining
cake layer. Quickly spoon and spread remaining
sherbet over top of cake. Cover; freeze 2 to 3
hours or overnight. To serve, let stand at room
temperature for about 10 minutes; cut cake into
1½-inch slices. Garnish as desired.

8 servings.

NUTRITION INFORMATION PER SERVING

SERVING SIZE: ⅛ OF RECIPE		PERCENT U.S. RDA PER SERVING	
Calories	250	Protein	6%
Protein	4 g	Vitamin A	*
Carbohydrate	55 g	Vitamin C	2%
Fat	2 g	Thiamine	4%
Cholesterol	7 mg	Riboflavin	8%
Sodium	160 mg	Niacin	2%
Potassium	135 mg	Calcium	6%
		Iron	2%

*Contains less than 2% of the U.S. RDA of this nutrient.

Pictured from top: Festive Fruit Salad with Lemon Yogurt Dressing, page 112; Italian Sandwich Loaf, page 113

Memorial Day Picnic

Serves 6
Chilled Wine and Sodas
Marinated Cocktail Mushrooms*
Assorted Crackers and Cheese Cubes
Broccoli Tortellini Salad*
and/or
Festive Fruit Salad with Lemon Yogurt Dressing*
Italian Sandwich Loaf*
No-Bake Bars*   Anise Toasties*
*Recipe included

Good friends, good food and good weather add up to one perfect picnic to herald summer's grand entrance. Everything seems to taste better in Mother Nature's dining room, and this menu adapts beautifully to patio or park setting.

Cornerstones of summer entertaining are fresh fruit and vegetables, minimal preparation time and versatile menus. Here, all three combine for a mouth-watering al fresco feast. The Festive Fruit Salad can double as salad or dessert, served with the bars, and the Italian Sandwich Loaf adapts to heating in home oven or on a grill at the park. Do-ahead steps give the Marinated Cocktail Mushrooms, Lemon Yogurt Dressing and Broccoli Tortellini Salad ample time for flavors to meld during refrigeration. For variety, substitute your favorite grilled entrees for the sandwich loaf. The rest of the menu complements any number of warm-weather recipes for meat, poultry or fish.

Just a reminder about food safety. If you plan to tote these and other foods, be sure to pack perishables in well-insulated containers. Hot foods should be kept hot and cold foods well chilled. Potentially dangerous bacteria growth can go undetected since taste, odor and appearance of affected foods do not change noticeably in just a few hours. Keep coolers in a shaded area and tightly closed until serving or reheating time.

Preparation Timetable

Day Before Picnic

Refrigerate wine and sodas • Prepare *Marinated Cocktail Mushrooms;* cover and refrigerate • Prepare *No-Bake Bars* and/or *Anise Toasties.*

Day of Picnic

Early in the Day: Prepare *Broccoli Tortellini Salad,* omitting tomatoes, olives and Parmesan cheese; cover and refrigerate • Prepare *Festive Fruit Salad with Lemon Yogurt Dressing,* combine fruit, omitting bananas, in nonmetal container and prepare dressing; cover each and refrigerate • Place crackers and cheese cubes in covered containers for toting.

Before Picnic: Prepare *Italian Sandwich Loaf;* heat in oven. Or securely wrap assembled sandwich in heavy-duty foil and place in cooler for toting; at picnic site, heat sandwich on grill • Add tomatoes to tortellini salad. Garnish with olives and sprinkle with Parmesan cheese; cover and place in cooler or refrigerator • Add sliced bananas to fruit salad; cover and place in cooler or refrigerator.

Marinated Cocktail Mushrooms

¼ cup white wine vinegar
¼ cup olive oil
2 tablespoons sugar
1 small onion, chopped
1 garlic clove, minced
1 (4.5-ounce) jar whole mushrooms, drained*

In nonmetal container, combine vinegar, oil, sugar, onion and garlic. Add mushrooms; mix well. Cover; refrigerate several hours or until serving time. Serve with toothpicks.
48 appetizers.

TIP: *If desired, 1 pound fresh mushrooms can be substituted for the jar of mushrooms. Wipe mushrooms with damp cloth or brush. Cook in boiling salted water for 10 minutes; drain. Continue as directed above.

NUTRITION INFORMATION PER SERVING
SERVING SIZE: 1 APPETIZER

		PERCENT U.S. RDA PER SERVING	
Calories	4	Protein	*
Protein	0 g	Vitamin A	*
Carbohydrate	0 g	Vitamin C	*
Fat	0 g	Thiamine	*
Cholesterol	0 mg	Riboflavin	*
Sodium	5 mg	Niacin	*
Potassium	0 mg	Calcium	*
		Iron	*

*Contains less than 2% of the U.S. RDA of this nutrient.

Festive Fruit Salad with Lemon Yogurt Dressing

LEMON YOGURT DRESSING

1 (8-ounce) carton lemon yogurt
1 tablespoon lemon juice
1 tablespoon honey

SALAD

1 kiwifruit, peeled, sliced
2 cups cubed cantaloupe
1 cup sliced strawberries
1 banana, sliced

In small bowl, combine all dressing ingredients; blend well. Cover; refrigerate to blend flavors. In large bowl, combine kiwifruit, cantaloupe and strawberries; toss gently. Cover; refrigerate until serving time. Just before serving, add sliced banana. Top each ⅔-cup serving of fruit mixture with 2 tablespoons dressing.
6 (⅔-cup) servings.

NUTRITION INFORMATION PER SERVING
SERVING SIZE: ⅔ CUP

		PERCENT U.S. RDA PER SERVING	
Calories	120	Protein	4%
Protein	3 g	Vitamin A	35%
Carbohydrate	24 g	Vitamin C	100%
Fat	1 g	Thiamine	2%
Cholesterol	2 mg	Riboflavin	8%
Sodium	30 mg	Niacin	2%
Potassium	430 mg	Calcium	6%
		Iron	2%

Broccoli Tortellini Salad

1 (7-ounce) package cheese tortellini
1 cup broccoli florets
½ cup finely chopped fresh parsley
1 tablespoon chopped pimiento
1 (6-ounce) jar marinated artichoke hearts, undrained
2 green onions, sliced
2½ teaspoons chopped fresh basil or ¼ teaspoon dried basil leaves
½ teaspoon garlic powder
½ cup prepared Italian dressing
5 to 6 cherry tomatoes, halved
   Sliced ripe olives, if desired
   Grated Parmesan cheese, if desired

Cook tortellini to desired doneness as directed on package. Drain; rinse with cold water.

In large bowl, combine all ingredients except cherry tomatoes, ripe olives and Parmesan cheese. Cover; refrigerate 4 to 6 hours to blend flavors. Just before serving, add tomatoes; mix lightly. Garnish with olives; sprinkle with Parmesan cheese.
6 (1-cup) servings.

TIP: Salad can be made a day ahead, omitting broccoli, tomatoes, olives and Parmesan cheese; cover and refrigerate. Add broccoli and tomatoes just before serving; garnish with olives and sprinkle with cheese.

NUTRITION INFORMATION PER SERVING
SERVING SIZE: 1 CUP

		PERCENT U.S. RDA PER SERVING	
Calories	280	Protein	10%
Protein	8 g	Vitamin A	20%
Carbohydrate	23 g	Vitamin C	40%
Fat	17 g	Thiamine	15%
Cholesterol	20 mg	Riboflavin	10%
Sodium	490 mg	Niacin	10%
Potassium	260 mg	Calcium	15%
		Iron	10%

Italian Sandwich Loaf

¾ pound ground Italian sausage
½ cup chopped green bell pepper
½ cup chopped onion
2 garlic cloves, minced
1 tablespoon olive oil
½ cup prepared spaghetti sauce
1 (4-ounce) can mushroom pieces and stems, drained
1 (1-pound) loaf Italian or French bread, cut in half lengthwise
4 ounces mozzarella cheese, sliced

In large skillet, cook sausage, green pepper, onion and garlic in oil until vegetables are tender and sausage is no longer pink; drain. Add spaghetti sauce and mushrooms; mix well. Simmer 10 to 15 minutes.

Heat oven to 350° F. Spoon sausage mixture onto bottom half of Italian bread; top with cheese and remaining bread half. Place on sheet of heavy-duty foil; wrap securely with double-fold seal. Bake at 350° F. for 15 to 20 minutes or until thoroughly heated. To serve, cut into 6 sandwiches. Garnish as desired.
6 sandwiches.

TIP: Sandwich loaf can be heated on grill. Prepare as directed above. Cook over medium-high coals for 15 to 20 minutes or until thoroughly heated.

NUTRITION INFORMATION PER SERVING

SERVING SIZE: 1 SANDWICH		PERCENT U.S. RDA PER SERVING	
Calories	410	Protein	30%
Protein	18 g	Vitamin A	8%
Carbohydrate	49 g	Vitamin C	10%
Fat	16 g	Thiamine	35%
Cholesterol	33 mg	Riboflavin	20%
Sodium	930 mg	Niacin	20%
Potassium	300 mg	Calcium	20%
		Iron	15%

No-Bake Bars

2 cups sugar
¼ cup unsweetened cocoa
½ cup milk
½ cup margarine or butter
1 cup peanut butter
1 teaspoon vanilla
2 cups quick-cooking rolled oats
1 cup shredded coconut

Lightly grease 13 × 9-inch pan. In large saucepan, combine sugar, cocoa, milk and margarine. Bring to a boil over medium heat, stirring constantly; remove from heat. Add peanut butter and vanilla; mix well. Stir in rolled oats and coconut. Spread in greased pan. Refrigerate until set. Cut into bars. Store in refrigerator.
36 bars.

MICROWAVE DIRECTIONS: Lightly grease 13 × 9-inch pan. Place margarine in 2-quart microwave-safe bowl. Microwave on HIGH for 60 seconds or until melted. Stir in sugar, cocoa and milk; mix well. Microwave on HIGH for 3½ to 4½ minutes or until mixture boils, stirring once halfway through cooking. Continue as directed above.

NUTRITION INFORMATION PER SERVING

SERVING SIZE: 1 BAR		PERCENT U.S. RDA PER SERVING	
Calories	140	Protein	4%
Protein	3 g	Vitamin A	2%
Carbohydrate	17 g	Vitamin C	*
Fat	7 g	Thiamine	2%
Cholesterol	0 mg	Riboflavin	*
Sodium	70 mg	Niacin	4%
Potassium	85 mg	Calcium	*
		Iron	2%

*Contains less than 2% of the U.S. RDA of this nutrient.

Anise Toasties

1 package pudding-included yellow cake mix
¾ cup oil
5 eggs
2 tablespoons anise seed
1 cup chopped almonds
Powdered sugar

Heat oven to 325° F. Grease and flour 15 × 10 × 1 or 17 × 11 × 1-inch baking pan. In large bowl, blend cake mix, oil and eggs at low speed until moistened; beat 2 minutes at high speed. Fold in anise seed and almonds. Spread in greased and floured pan.

Bake at 325° F. for 25 to 35 minutes or until golden brown. Cool 10 minutes. With sharp knife, cut 3 equal strips lengthwise; cut 12 strips crosswise, forming 36 bars. Place bars 2 inches apart on ungreased cookie sheets. Increase oven temperature to 350° F. and bake for 8 to 12 minutes or until cut sides begin to toast. Immediately remove from cookie sheets; cool 10 minutes. Sprinkle with powdered sugar. Cool completely. Store loosely covered.
36 bars.

HIGH ALTITUDE—Above 3500 Feet: Decrease oil to ½ cup. Bake as directed above.

NUTRITION INFORMATION PER SERVING

SERVING SIZE: 1 BAR		PERCENT U.S. RDA PER SERVING	
Calories	140	Protein	2%
Protein	2 g	Vitamin A	*
Carbohydrate	13 g	Vitamin C	*
Fat	9 g	Thiamine	2%
Cholesterol	30 mg	Riboflavin	4%
Sodium	100 mg	Niacin	2%
Potassium	45 mg	Calcium	4%
		Iron	2%

*Contains less than 2% of the U.S. RDA of this nutrient.

Pictured top to bottom: Marinated Tomato Toss, page 116; Flaky Butter Brioches, page 117; Honey-Glazed Carrots, page 117; Salmon Steaks with Spinach Sauce, page 116

Father's Day Dinner

Serves 6
Chilled Wine and Fruit Juices
Creamy Brie Spread*
Assorted Crackers, Melba Toast or Cracker Bread
Marinated Tomato Toss*   *Flaky Butter Brioches**
Salmon Steaks with Spinach Sauce*
Honey-Glazed Carrots*
Chocolate Strawberry Pie*
Coffee   Tea
*Recipe included

The first Father's Day (a woman's idea, by the way) was celebrated back in 1910. However, it wasn't until 1936 that the third Sunday in June officially was set aside to honor Dads across the land. Since this holiday is very much a family celebration, what better way to fete father than with a delicious home-cooked meal with all the dash of fine dining?

The recipes are a pleasant choice for warm weather—on the lighter side, but substantial enough to satisfy. And the colorful medley of salmon, tomatoes, carrots and ruby red strawberries, all in their prime, ensures beautiful presentation. While Dad is opening cards and gifts, gather around to savor the Creamy Brie Spread—delightful with icy cold fruit juices or wine garnished with lemon twists. The vivid Marinated Tomato Toss can be enjoyed as a relaxed first course while the salmon is poaching or can be served with the entree. With today's busy schedules, unhurried family gatherings have become a luxury. Certainly it is that unique feeling of luxury that you want to convey today.

The decadently rich dessert is "simple as pie" to make but has the aura of hours of preparation. Serve it with fresh brewed coffee or a special dessert coffee topped with a fluff of whipped cream as a grand finale for a grand day.

Preparation Timetable

Several Days Ahead
Prepare *Flaky Butter Brioches;* cool completely, wrap in foil and freeze.

Day Before Dinner
Refrigerate wine and fruit juices • Prepare *Creamy Brie Spread;* cover and refrigerate • Marinate tomatoes and prepare croutons for *Marinated Tomato Toss* • Cut up carrots for *Honey-Glazed Carrots;* place in plastic bag and refrigerate.

Day of Dinner
Early in the Day: Remove brioches from freezer to thaw • Prepare *Chocolate Strawberry Pie;* refrigerate.

Shortly Before Serving: Unmold brie spread and garnish with almonds; arrange crackers, melba toast or cracker bread on tray • Warm foil-wrapped brioches in oven • Prepare coffee and/or tea • Combine and toss all ingredients for tomato salad • Prepare glazed carrots; keep warm • Prepare *Salmon Steaks with Spinach Sauce.*

Creamy Brie Spread

4 ounces Brie cheese, softened
1 (3-ounce) package cream cheese, softened
½ teaspoon seasoned salt
2 tablespoons sliced almonds
  Assorted crackers, melba toast or cracker bread

Line 10-ounce custard cup or bowl with plastic wrap. In medium bowl, blend Brie (including crust), cream cheese and seasoned salt until smooth. Spoon into lined cup; press firmly to pack. Cover; refrigerate several hours or overnight to blend flavors. Unmold onto serving plate; remove plastic wrap. Press almonds on top and sides of cheese mold. Serve with assorted crackers, melba toast or cracker bread.
1¼ cups.

NUTRITION INFORMATION PER SERVING
SERVING SIZE: 1 TABLESPOON SPREAD / PERCENT U.S. RDA PER SERVING

Calories	35	Protein	2%
Protein	2 g	Vitamin A	*
Carbohydrate	0 g	Vitamin C	*
Fat	3 g	Thiamine	*
Cholesterol	10 mg	Riboflavin	2%
Sodium	90 mg	Niacin	*
Potassium	20 mg	Calcium	*
		Iron	*

*Contains less than 2% of the U.S. RDA of this nutrient.

Marinated Tomato Toss

MARINADE
¼ cup oil
1 tablespoon sugar
3 tablespoons vinegar
2 teaspoons finely chopped fresh parsley
1 teaspoon finely chopped green onions
⅛ teaspoon garlic salt
⅛ teaspoon dried basil leaves
  Dash dried oregano leaves
  Dash pepper
12 cherry tomatoes, cut in half

CROUTONS
3 tablespoons butter or margarine
2 slices day-old bread, cut into 1-inch squares
1 garlic clove, minced
⅛ teaspoon dried thyme leaves, crushed

4 cups torn salad greens
2 ounces Swiss cheese slices, cut into julienne strips

In medium bowl, combine all marinade ingredients except tomatoes; blend well. Gently stir in tomatoes. Cover; refrigerate at least 8 hours or overnight.

In small skillet, melt butter, add bread squares, garlic and thyme. Cook over medium-low heat until croutons are light brown and crisp, stirring frequently.

Just before serving, lightly toss salad greens, cheese, marinated tomatoes and croutons with enough of the marinade to moisten greens. Arrange on chilled salad plates.
6 (1¼-cup) servings.

NUTRITION INFORMATION PER SERVING
SERVING SIZE: 1¼ CUPS / PERCENT U.S. RDA PER SERVING

Calories	220	Protein	6%
Protein	4 g	Vitamin A	20%
Carbohydrate	10 g	Vitamin C	15%
Fat	18 g	Thiamine	4%
Cholesterol	24 mg	Riboflavin	4%
Sodium	170 mg	Niacin	2%
Potassium	170 mg	Calcium	10%
		Iron	4%

Salmon Steaks with Spinach Sauce

2 cups chicken broth
3 tablespoons finely chopped onion
3 tablespoons finely chopped fresh parsley
¼ teaspoon salt
1 bay leaf
6 salmon steaks (about 2 pounds)
¾ cup whipping cream
3 egg yolks, beaten
1 (10-ounce) package frozen chopped spinach, cooked, well drained
1 tablespoon lemon juice

In large skillet, combine chicken broth, onion, parsley, salt and bay leaf; bring to a boil. Add salmon; cover and simmer over low heat 8 to 10 minutes or until salmon flakes easily with fork. Place salmon on serving plate; keep warm. Remove bay leaf.

Boil broth mixture until reduced to about 1 cup. In small bowl, combine cream and egg yolks; blend well. Slowly stir about half of broth mixture into cream mixture. Stir cream mixture into remaining broth mixture. Cook over low heat until thickened and bubbly, stirring constantly. Stir in spinach and lemon juice; heat thoroughly. If desired, blend sauce in food processor or blender until smooth. Serve with salmon steaks.
6 servings.

NUTRITION INFORMATION PER SERVING
SERVING SIZE: ⅙ OF RECIPE / PERCENT U.S. RDA PER SERVING

Calories	370	Protein	50%
Protein	35 g	Vitamin A	35%
Carbohydrate	4 g	Vitamin C	15%
Fat	24 g	Thiamine	25%
Cholesterol	233 mg	Riboflavin	45%
Sodium	520 mg	Niacin	70%
Potassium	1100 mg	Calcium	10%
		Iron	15%

Flaky Butter Brioches

4¼ to 4¾ cups all purpose or unbleached flour
⅓ cup sugar
1 teaspoon salt
2 packages active dry yeast
1¼ cups milk
½ cup butter or margarine
3 eggs

Generously grease 24 individual brioche pans or muffin cups. Lightly spoon flour into measuring cup; level off. In large bowl, combine 2 cups flour, sugar, salt and yeast; blend well. In small saucepan, heat milk and butter until very warm (120 to 130° F.). Add warm liquid and 2 of the eggs to flour mixture. Blend at low speed until moistened; beat 3 minutes at medium speed. By hand, stir in an additional 2 to 2¼ cups flour until dough pulls cleanly away from sides of bowl.

On floured surface, knead in ¼ to ½ cup flour until dough is smooth, about 2 to 3 minutes. Divide dough into 4 equal parts. Shape 3 dough parts into 8 balls each. Place 1 ball in each greased pan. Shape remaining dough into 24 small balls. With finger, make deep indentation in center of each large ball. Place 1 small ball in each indentation, pressing down slightly. Cover; let rise in warm place (80 to 85° F.) until light and doubled in size, about 45 minutes.

Heat oven to 350° F. Beat remaining egg; carefully brush over rolls. Bake at 350° F. for 15 to 20 minutes or until golden brown. Immediately remove from pans.
24 rolls.

HIGH ALTITUDE—Above 3500 feet: No change.

NUTRITION INFORMATION PER SERVING
SERVING SIZE: 1 ROLL

		PERCENT U.S. RDA PER SERVING	
Calories	150	Protein	6%
Protein	4 g	Vitamin A	4%
Carbohydrate	23 g	Vitamin C	*
Fat	5 g	Thiamine	15%
Cholesterol	38 mg	Riboflavin	10%
Sodium	140 mg	Niacin	8%
Potassium	65 mg	Calcium	2%
		Iron	6%

*Contains less than 2% of the U.S. RDA of this nutrient.

Honey-Glazed Carrots

⅓ cup water
¼ teaspoon salt
1 pound fresh carrots, cut into 2½ × ¼-inch strips
2 tablespoons butter or margarine
2 tablespoons honey

In medium saucepan, combine water and salt; bring to a boil. Add carrots. Cover and cook over medium heat until carrots are tender, about 8 to 12 minutes; drain. Melt butter in large skillet; stir in honey. Add carrots; cook over low heat until carrots are well glazed, stirring constantly.
6 (⅔-cup) servings.

NUTRITION INFORMATION PER SERVING
SERVING SIZE: ⅔ CUP

		PERCENT U.S. RDA PER SERVING	
Calories	90	Protein	*
Protein	1 g	Vitamin A	390%
Carbohydrate	13 g	Vitamin C	8%
Fat	4 g	Thiamine	4%
Cholesterol	10 mg	Riboflavin	2%
Sodium	150 mg	Niacin	2%
Potassium	230 mg	Calcium	2%
		Iron	2%

*Contains less than 2% of the U.S. RDA of this nutrient.

Chocolate Strawberry Pie

1 (15-ounce) package refrigerated pie crusts

FILLING
1 (6-ounce) package (1 cup) semi-sweet chocolate chips
2 tablespoons margarine or butter
¼ cup powdered sugar
3 tablespoons cherry-flavored liqueur or water
1 (8-ounce) package cream cheese, softened
1½ to 2 pints whole strawberries

GLAZE
3 tablespoons red currant jelly
2 teaspoons cherry-flavored liqueur or water

Heat oven to 450° F. Prepare pie crust according to package directions for *unfilled one-crust pie* using 9-inch pie pan or 10-inch tart pan with removable bottom. (Refrigerate remaining crust for later use as desired.) Place prepared crust in pan; press in bottom and up sides of pan. Flute or trim edges if necessary. Bake at 450° F. for 9 to 11 minutes or until lightly browned. Cool.

In medium saucepan, melt chocolate chips and margarine, stirring constantly. Stir in powdered sugar, 3 tablespoons liqueur and cream cheese; blend well. Pour into cooled crust. Arrange strawberries over chocolate mixture. In small saucepan, heat jelly with 2 teaspoons liqueur until warm; spoon or brush over strawberries. Refrigerate at least 2 hours or until serving time.
8 servings.

NUTRITION INFORMATION PER SERVING
SERVING SIZE: ⅛ OF RECIPE

		PERCENT U.S. RDA PER SERVING	
Calories	450	Protein	6%
Protein	4 g	Vitamin A	10%
Carbohydrate	45 g	Vitamin C	50%
Fat	28 g	Thiamine	*
Cholesterol	39 mg	Riboflavin	8%
Sodium	230 mg	Niacin	*
Potassium	260 mg	Calcium	4%
		Iron	8%

*Contains less than 2% of the U.S. RDA of this nutrient.

Pictured clockwise from left: Frozen Coleslaw, page 120; Crispy Herbed Chicken, page 120; Slow-Cooker Beans, page 121

Fourth of July Family Reunion

Serves 10 to 13
Assorted Chilled Sodas
Frozen Coleslaw*
Glorified Rice*
Barbecued Beef Sandwiches*
Crispy Herbed Chicken*
Slow-Cooker Beans*
Stars 'n Stripes Cookie Squares*
*Recipe included

A family reunion is a red-letter day on anyone's calendar. Why not make that red, white and blue and turn it into a fabulous Fourth celebration? Fun for all is guaranteed with a swim before eating and the perfect follow-up—fireworks at the city park.

With plenty of outdoor games and activities the entertainment is built right into this all-American holiday, so you can turn your attention to planning a hearty down-home spread. If your family get-together is like most, appetites come in all sizes and guests in all ages. So you want a sumptuous sampler of easy-to-eat foods that will appeal to everyone.

No need for you to do all the cooking with recipes like Frozen Coleslaw and Glorified Rice, so simple to tote. You can provide copies of the recipes and invite family members to prepare and bring one. If the group is large, consider doubling the recipes or asking several people to bring the same thing.

Paper or plastic plates in flag colors are a perfect complement to this patriotic occasion. Toy drums surrounded by small flags make great centerpieces for the picnic tables. Fruit-topped Stars 'n Stripes Cookie Squares provide a colorful finale. And be sure to have plenty of balloons, crepe paper and tape on hand for the kids to do some of their own picnic table decorations.

Preparation Timetable

Several Days Ahead
Prepare *Frozen Coleslaw;* cover and freeze.

Day Before Reunion
Refrigerate sodas.

Day of Reunion
Early in the Day: Remove coleslaw from freezer and thaw in refrigerator until serving time • Prepare *Glorified Rice;* cover and refrigerate • Prepare *Stars 'n Stripes Cookie Squares;* refrigerate • Prepare *Slow-Cooker Beans.*

Before Serving: Prepare filling *for Barbecued Beef Sandwiches;* keep warm • Prepare *Crispy Herbed Chicken;* keep warm.

Frozen Coleslaw

1 large green cabbage, finely shredded (8 cups)
1 teaspoon salt
2 medium carrots, shredded (1 cup)
1 cup chopped celery
½ cup chopped green bell pepper
¼ cup chopped green onions

DRESSING
1½ cups sugar
¾ cup white or cider vinegar
1 teaspoon celery seed
1 teaspoon mustard seed
1 teaspoon salt

In large bowl, sprinkle cabbage with salt. Let stand 1 hour; drain thoroughly. Stir in carrots, celery, green pepper and onions; set aside.

In medium saucepan, combine all dressing ingredients. Bring to a boil; boil 1 minute. Pour dressing over vegetables; toss until well coated. Store in freezer containers for up to 1 month.

To serve, thaw in refrigerator for up to 24 hours, depending on size of container. Serve slightly frozen.

14 (½-cup) servings.

NUTRITION INFORMATION PER SERVING
SERVING SIZE: ½ CUP

			PERCENT U.S. RDA PER SERVING
Calories	110	Protein	*
Protein	1 g	Vitamin A	45%
Carbohydrate	26 g	Vitamin C	40%
Fat	0 g	Thiamine	2%
Cholesterol	0 mg	Riboflavin	*
Sodium	320 mg	Niacin	*
Potassium	170 mg	Calcium	2%
		Iron	2%

*Contains less than 2% of the U.S. RDA of this nutrient.

Barbecued Beef Sandwiches

4 cups shredded cooked beef
¼ cup firmly packed brown sugar
1 tablespoon dry mustard
¼ teaspoon pepper
1½ cups water
¼ cup vinegar
¼ cup margarine or butter
½ teaspoon salt
1 cup ketchup
1 tablespoon Worcestershire sauce
12 onion flavored hamburger buns

In large skillet, combine beef, brown sugar, mustard, pepper, water, vinegar and margarine. Bring to a boil. Cover; reduce heat and simmer 20 minutes. Add salt, ketchup and Worcestershire sauce. Simmer uncovered 20 to 25 minutes or until of desired consistency. Spoon ⅓ cup hot filling on buns.

12 servings.

NUTRITION INFORMATION PER SERVING
SERVING SIZE: 1/12 OF RECIPE

			PERCENT U.S. RDA PER SERVING
Calories	300	Protein	30%
Protein	19 g	Vitamin A	8%
Carbohydrate	32 g	Vitamin C	4%
Fat	11 g	Thiamine	15%
Cholesterol	47 mg	Riboflavin	15%
Sodium	640 mg	Niacin	20%
Potassium	310 mg	Calcium	4%
		Iron	15%

Crispy Herbed Chicken

2 cups mashed potato flakes
⅔ cup grated Parmesan cheese
2 tablespoons parsley flakes
1 teaspoon onion powder
½ teaspoon garlic salt
¼ teaspoon paprika
⅛ to ¼ teaspoon pepper
3 whole chickens, quartered, skinned, rinsed and patted dry
1 cup margarine or butter, melted

Heat oven to 375° F. Grease or line with foil two 15 × 10 × 1-inch baking pans or two 13 × 9-inch pans. In medium bowl, combine potato flakes, Parmesan cheese, parsley flakes, onion powder, garlic salt, paprika and pepper; mix well. Dip chicken pieces in margarine; roll in potato-flake mixture to coat. Place in greased pans. Bake at 375° F. for 60 to 75 minutes or until chicken is tender and golden brown.*

12 servings.

TIP: *For even browning, switch position of pans halfway through baking.

NUTRITION INFORMATION PER SERVING
SERVING SIZE: 1/12 OF RECIPE

			PERCENT U.S. RDA PER SERVING
Calories	400	Protein	50%
Protein	35 g	Vitamin A	15%
Carbohydrate	8 g	Vitamin C	*
Fat	25 g	Thiamine	4%
Cholesterol	102 mg	Riboflavin	15%
Sodium	470 mg	Niacin	50%
Potassium	360 mg	Calcium	10%
		Iron	8%

*Contains less than 2% of the U.S. RDA of this nutrient.

Slow-Cooker Beans

½ pound bacon, diced
½ cup firmly packed brown sugar
¼ cup cornstarch
1 teaspoon dry mustard
½ cup molasses
1 tablespoon vinegar
4 (16-ounce) cans pork and beans
1 medium onion, chopped
1 green bell pepper, chopped

In medium skillet, fry bacon until crisp. Drain, reserving 2 tablespoons drippings. In slow cooker, combine bacon, drippings and remaining ingredients, stirring until well mixed. Cook uncovered on HIGH heat for 1 hour. Cover; reduce heat to LOW and cook for 3 to 4 hours longer.

18 (½-cup) servings.

NUTRITION INFORMATION PER SERVING
SERVING SIZE: ½ CUP

		PERCENT U.S. RDA PER SERVING	
Calories	200	Protein	10%
Protein	6 g	Vitamin A	4%
Carbohydrate	34 g	Vitamin C	8%
Fat	5 g	Thiamine	6%
Cholesterol	11 mg	Riboflavin	2%
Sodium	480 mg	Niacin	4%
Potassium	460 mg	Calcium	8%
		Iron	15%

Glorified Rice

3 cups cold cooked rice*
1 large tart apple, chopped (1 cup)
⅓ cup sugar
½ teaspoon salt
2 cups whipping cream, whipped, or 4 cups frozen whipped topping, thawed
1 teaspoon vanilla
½ teaspoon almond extract
1 (20-ounce) can crushed pineapple, drained
1 (10-ounce) jar (1 cup) maraschino cherries, drained, quartered

In large bowl, combine all ingredients; mix well. Cover and refrigerate until serving time.

12 (⅔-cup) servings.

TIP: *For lighter, fluffier rice, add 1 teaspoon lemon juice to the cooking water.

NUTRITION INFORMATION PER SERVING
SERVING SIZE: ⅔ CUP

		PERCENT U.S. RDA PER SERVING	
Calories	270	Protein	4%
Protein	2 g	Vitamin A	10%
Carbohydrate	31 g	Vitamin C	6%
Fat	15 g	Thiamine	8%
Cholesterol	54 mg	Riboflavin	2%
Sodium	105 mg	Niacin	4%
Potassium	120 mg	Calcium	4%
		Iron	4%

Stars 'n Stripes Cookie Squares

1 (20-ounce) package refrigerated sliceable sugar cookie dough
1 (8-ounce) package cream cheese, softened
3 cups powdered sugar
1 teaspoon grated lemon or orange peel
50 blueberries (about ½ cup)
2 cups raspberries
2 tablespoons apple jelly, if desired

Heat oven to 375° F. Line 15 × 10 × 1-inch pan with foil. Slice cookie dough into ¼-inch slices; place in foil-lined pan. With lightly floured hands, press dough over bottom to form crust. Bake at 375° F. for 10 to 15 minutes or until golden brown. Cool completely; remove from foil. Place on serving tray.

In small bowl, beat cream cheese, powdered sugar and lemon peel until smooth. Spread over cookie crust. Arrange berries over cream cheese mixture to resemble flag, using 50 blueberries in upper left corner for stars and raspberries arranged in 7 rows to form stripes. Melt jelly in small saucepan over low heat; brush gently over fruit. Refrigerate until serving time. Cut into squares to serve.

12 servings.

NUTRITION INFORMATION PER SERVING
SERVING SIZE: ¹/₁₂ OF RECIPE

		PERCENT U.S. RDA PER SERVING	
Calories	390	Protein	6%
Protein	4 g	Vitamin A	6%
Carbohydrate	59 g	Vitamin C	10%
Fat	15 g	Thiamine	8%
Cholesterol	21 mg	Riboflavin	10%
Sodium	260 mg	Niacin	6%
Potassium	85 mg	Calcium	2%
		Iron	6%

Pictured clockwise from top left: Dilled Garden Dip, page 125; Cheese-Stuffed Pepper Wedges, page 124; Bacon-Filled Cherry Tomatoes, page 124; Crunchy Cucumber Rounds, page 124; Peppy Party Onions, page 126

Labor Day "From-the-Garden" Get-Together

Serves 12 to 24
Chilled Wine, Sparkling Waters and Sodas
Crunchy Cucumber Rounds*
Cheese-Stuffed Pepper Wedges*
Cheesy Zucchini Canapés*
Bacon-Filled Cherry Tomatoes*
Dilled Garden Dip*   Assorted Cut-up Fresh Vegetables
Tangy Ham 'n Avocado Crescents*
Spinach Surprise Bites*   Savory Mustard Sauce*
Assorted Crackers or Thinly Sliced Snack Rye Bread
Tangy Shrimp-Topped Cauliflower*
Peppy Party Onions*
Zucchini-Date Cake*   Orange-Carrot Cake*
*Recipe included

*H*ere's a dandy menu to showcase the tasty results of a summer of nurturing your vegetable garden. Just the ticket for an end-of-summer block party, an informal welcoming of new neighbors or just a gathering of green-thumbed friends who enjoy gardening as much as you do.

Ingredients could not be fresher or more abundant, from your own yard or a local farm produce stand. Preparation doesn't get much easier, particularly if you turn the party into a cooperative venture. Invite every guest to tote a tidbit or two to share according to his or her gardening specialty or culinary talent. Friends with an abundance of zucchini will be delighted to bake a few into moist, flavorful Zucchini-Date Cake. Assign cucumber, tomato and pepper treats to someone who has a garden filled with more of each than he or she can use. And, depending on the number of guests, you may want to suggest doubling some recipes in this menu such as the Dilled Garden Dip or Peppy Party Onions. Before you know it, the party will almost take care of itself.

For convenience, we suggest that the host supply the warm-from-the-oven Tangy Ham 'n Avocado Crescents and the Cheesy Zucchini Canapés in addition to ice-filled chests of chilled beverages.

Preparation Timetable

Day Before Party

Refrigerate wine coolers, sparkling waters, and sodas • Prepare *Zucchini-Date Cake* and *Orange-Carrot Cake;* cover and refrigerate • Prepare *Dilled Garden Dip;* cover and refrigerate • Cut up assorted fresh vegetables to be served with dips; place in plastic bags and refrigerate.

Day of Party

Early in the Day: Prepare *Spinach Surprise Bites, Savory Mustard Sauce, Tangy Shrimp-Topped Cauliflower, Peppy Party Onions* and *Bacon-Filled Cherry Tomatoes;* cover and refrigerate.

Several Hours Before: Prepare *Crunchy Cucumber Rounds* and *Cheese-Stuffed Pepper Wedges;* cover and refrigerate.

Shortly Before Serving: Arrange crackers or snack rye bread on tray • Prepare *Tangy Ham 'n Avocado Crescents* and *Cheesy Zucchini Canapés.*

Crunchy Cucumber Rounds

1 medium apple, finely chopped (1 cup)
½ cup crushed pineapple, well drained
¼ cup finely chopped pecans or nuts
¼ cup dairy sour cream
   Dash salt
3 medium cucumbers, chilled

In small bowl, combine all ingredients except cucumbers; mix well. Cover; refrigerate. Draw tines of fork lengthwise through cucumber peel to score; cut into slices ¼-inch thick. Dry on paper towels. Spoon about a teaspoonful of fruit mixture onto each cucumber slice. Garnish as desired. Serve immediately or cover and refrigerate up to 2 hours.
About 48 appetizers.

NUTRITION INFORMATION PER SERVING

SERVING SIZE: 1 APPETIZER		PERCENT U.S. RDA PER SERVING	
Calories	12	Protein	*
Protein	0 g	Vitamin A	*
Carbohydrate	1 g	Vitamin C	2%
Fat	1 g	Thiamine	*
Cholesterol	1 mg	Riboflavin	*
Sodium	0 mg	Niacin	*
Potassium	35 mg	Calcium	*
		Iron	*

*Contains less than 2% of the U.S. RDA of this nutrient.

Cheese-Stuffed Pepper Wedges

3 green or red bell peppers
1 (5-ounce) jar pimiento spread
1 (2¼-ounce) can deviled ham, drained
   Decorating bag and tips

Remove seeds and veins from peppers. Cut each pepper into 6 wedges; cut wedges in half crosswise. In small bowl, combine pimiento spread and deviled ham; stir until well blended. Attach desired tip to decorating bag; fill bag with filling. Pipe filling onto pepper wedges. Garnish as desired. Refrigerate until serving time.
36 appetizers.

NUTRITION INFORMATION PER SERVING

SERVING SIZE: 1 APPETIZER		PERCENT U.S. RDA PER SERVING	
Calories	18	Protein	*
Protein	1 g	Vitamin A	*
Carbohydrate	1 g	Vitamin C	10%
Fat	1 g	Thiamine	*
Cholesterol	3 mg	Riboflavin	*
Sodium	75 mg	Niacin	*
Potassium	25 mg	Calcium	2%
		Iron	*

*Contains less than 2% of the U.S. RDA of this nutrient.

Cheesy Zucchini Canapés

1 medium zucchini (about 6 inches long)
2 tablespoons margarine or butter, melted
   Chopped fresh basil or dried basil leaves
2 ounces thinly sliced ham, cut into 1-inch squares
2 ounces (½-cup) shredded mozzarella cheese

Cut zucchini into 24 (¼-inch-thick) slices; place on greased cookie sheet. Brush with margarine; sprinkle with basil. Top zucchini with ham; sprinkle with cheese. Broil about 6 inches from heat for 2 to 3 minutes or until cheese is hot and bubbly. Serve warm.
24 appetizers.

NUTRITION INFORMATION PER SERVING

SERVING SIZE: 1 APPETIZER		PERCENT U.S. RDA PER SERVING	
Calories	30	Protein	2%
Protein	1 g	Vitamin A	2%
Carbohydrate	1 g	Vitamin C	2%
Fat	2 g	Thiamine	*
Cholesterol	3 mg	Riboflavin	*
Sodium	55 mg	Niacin	*
Potassium	50 mg	Calcium	2%
		Iron	*

*Contains less than 2% of the U.S. RDA of this nutrient.

Bacon-Filled Cherry Tomatoes

1 pound bacon, crisply cooked, crumbled
¼ cup finely chopped green onions
2 tablespoons chopped fresh parsley
2 tablespoons grated Parmesan cheese
½ cup mayonnaise
24 cherry tomatoes

In medium bowl, combine all ingredients except cherry tomatoes; mix well. Remove stems from tomatoes. Place tomatoes stem side down on cutting board. Cut thin slice off top (opposite stem end) of each tomato. With small spoon or melon scoop, carefully hollow out tomato, leaving ⅛-inch-thick shell. Invert tomatoes on paper towels to drain. Fill tomatoes with bacon mixture. Garnish as desired. Cover loosely; refrigerate several hours to blend flavors.
24 appetizers.

NUTRITION INFORMATION PER SERVING

SERVING SIZE: 1 APPETIZER		PERCENT U.S. RDA PER SERVING	
Calories	70	Protein	2%
Protein	2 g	Vitamin A	2%
Carbohydrate	1 g	Vitamin C	8%
Fat	7 g	Thiamine	2%
Cholesterol	8 mg	Riboflavin	*
Sodium	120 mg	Niacin	2%
Potassium	60 mg	Calcium	*
		Iron	*

*Contains less than 2% of the U.S. RDA of this nutrient.

Dilled Garden Dip

1 (12-ounce) carton (1½ cups) creamed cottage
    cheese
1 tablespoon lemon juice
2 tablespoons shredded carrot
1 tablespoon sliced green onions
1 tablespoon chopped fresh parsley
1½ teaspoons chopped fresh dill weed or ½
    teaspoon dried dill weed
1 teaspoon sugar
    Dash pepper
    Cut-up fresh vegetables

In blender container, combine cottage cheese and
lemon juice. Cover; blend at medium speed for 3
to 5 minutes or until smooth. Stir in remaining
ingredients except cut-up vegetables. Cover;
refrigerate several hours or overnight to blend
flavors. Garnish as desired. Serve with cut-up
fresh vegetables.

1½ cups.

NUTRITION INFORMATION PER SERVING
SERVING SIZE: 1
TABLESPOON DIP

		PERCENT U.S. RDA PER SERVING	
Calories	20	Protein	2%
Protein	2 g	Vitamin A	4%
Carbohydrate	1 g	Vitamin C	*
Fat	1 g	Thiamine	*
Cholesterol	2 mg	Riboflavin	*
Sodium	60 mg	Niacin	*
Potassium	15 mg	Calcium	*
		Iron	*

*Contains less than 2% of the U.S. RDA of this nutrient.

Tangy Ham 'n Avocado Crescents

2 (8-ounce) cans refrigerated crescent dinner
    rolls
8 teaspoons horseradish mustard
8 thin slices boiled ham
2 (6-ounce) packages Swiss cheese slices
2 avocados, peeled, cut into 16 wedges

Heat oven to 375° F. Separate dough into 8
rectangles. Spread 1 teaspoon mustard on each
rectangle; top with 1 ham and 1 cheese slice. Cut
each rectangle into 2 triangles. Place 1 avocado
wedge on shortest side of each triangle. Roll up,
starting at shortest side and rolling to opposite
point. Place point side down on ungreased cookie
sheets. Bake at 375° F. for 12 to 17 minutes or
until golden brown. Serve warm.

16 sandwiches.

NUTRITION INFORMATION PER SERVING
SERVING SIZE: 1
SANDWICH

		PERCENT U.S. RDA PER SERVING	
Calories	240	Protein	15%
Protein	10 g	Vitamin A	6%
Carbohydrate	14 g	Vitamin C	4%
Fat	16 g	Thiamine	10%
Cholesterol	26 mg	Riboflavin	10%
Sodium	380 mg	Niacin	8%
Potassium	270 mg	Calcium	20%
		Iron	6%

Spinach Surprise Bites

24 small fresh spinach leaves (¼ pound)
1 quart boiling water
4 ounces cooked ham, cut into 24 cubes

Wash spinach thoroughly; remove stems. Place
spinach leaves in colander or large strainer. Pour
boiling water over spinach; let stand 2 to 3
minutes. Rinse with cold water; drain thoroughly.
Place spinach leaves on paper towel; blot excess
moisture.

Place 1 ham cube at stem end of each spinach
leaf. Roll ham cube inside leaf, folding in sides;
secure with toothpick. Place appetizers on serving
plate. Cover; refrigerate up to 4 hours or until
serving time. Serve with Savory Mustard Sauce
(this page), if desired.

24 appetizers.

NUTRITION INFORMATION PER SERVING
SERVING SIZE: 1
APPETIZER

		PERCENT U.S. RDA PER SERVING	
Calories	8	Protein	*
Protein	1 g	Vitamin A	6%
Carbohydrate	0 g	Vitamin C	4%
Fat	0 g	Thiamine	2%
Cholesterol	3 mg	Riboflavin	*
Sodium	60 mg	Niacin	*
Potassium	40 mg	Calcium	*
		Iron	*

*Contains less than 2% of the U.S. RDA of this nutrient.

Savory Mustard Sauce

2 to 4 tablespoons dry mustard*
2 tablespoons sugar
⅛ teaspoon onion powder
¼ cup cider vinegar
1 egg, slightly beaten
½ cup mayonnaise or salad dressing

In small saucepan, combine mustard, sugar and
onion powder. Stir in vinegar and egg; blend
well. Cook over low heat until mixture begins to
thicken. Continue to cook an additional 3
minutes, stirring constantly. Refrigerate 10 to 15
minutes until cool. Stir in mayonnaise. Store in
refrigerator.

1 cup.

TIP: *The amount of dry mustard determines the
hotness of the sauce.

NUTRITION INFORMATION PER SERVING
SERVING SIZE: ½
TEASPOON

		PERCENT U.S. RDA PER SERVING	
Calories	10	Protein	*
Protein	0 g	Vitamin A	*
Carbohydrate	0 g	Vitamin C	*
Fat	1 g	Thiamine	*
Cholesterol	3 mg	Riboflavin	*
Sodium	5 mg	Niacin	*
Potassium	0 mg	Calcium	*
		Iron	*

*Contains less than 2% of the U.S. RDA of this nutrient.

Tangy Shrimp-Topped Cauliflower

1 cup water
1 tablespoon lemon juice
1 medium head cauliflower, leaves removed,
    stem trimmed
    Romaine or leaf lettuce
½ cup mayonnaise
1 teaspoon prepared mustard
1 (4-ounce) can medium shrimp, drained,
    rinsed
    Chopped fresh or dried dill weed, if desired

In large saucepan, bring water and lemon juice to a boil. Add cauliflower; reduce heat. Cover and simmer until tender, about 15 to 20 minutes. Drain well; refrigerate until cold.

Place chilled cauliflower, stem side down, on lettuce-lined shallow serving dish or platter. In small bowl, combine mayonnaise and mustard; spread evenly over top of cauliflower. Arrange shrimp over mayonnaise mixture. Sprinkle with dill weed. Cover loosely; refrigerate until serving time. To serve, have guests carefully spoon florets with sauce and shrimp onto plate.

12 servings.

NUTRITION INFORMATION PER SERVING
SERVING SIZE: 1/12 OF RECIPE

		PERCENT U.S. RDA PER SERVING	
Calories	90	Protein	4%
Protein	3 g	Vitamin A	2%
Carbohydrate	2 g	Vitamin C	35%
Fat	8 g	Thiamine	*
Cholesterol	24 mg	Riboflavin	*
Sodium	80 mg	Niacin	2%
Potassium	140 mg	Calcium	*
		Iron	4%

*Contains less than 2% of the U.S. RDA of this nutrient.

Peppy Party Onions

1 (3-ounce) package cream cheese, softened
1 tablespoon mayonnaise
¼ teaspoon chili powder
3 drops hot pepper sauce
12 small green onions, trimmed, patted dry
2 ounces (½ cup) finely shredded Cheddar
    cheese

In small bowl, combine cream cheese, mayonnaise, chili powder and hot pepper sauce; blend well. Spread white portion of each onion generously with cream cheese mixture. Roll in Cheddar cheese. Cover; refrigerate until set.

12 appetizers.

NUTRITION INFORMATION PER SERVING
SERVING SIZE: 1 APPETIZER

		PERCENT U.S. RDA PER SERVING	
Calories	60	Protein	2%
Protein	2 g	Vitamin A	4%
Carbohydrate	1 g	Vitamin C	4%
Fat	5 g	Thiamine	*
Cholesterol	13 mg	Riboflavin	2%
Sodium	60 mg	Niacin	*
Potassium	55 mg	Calcium	4%
		Iron	*

*Contains less than 2% of the U.S. RDA of this nutrient.

Orange-Carrot Cake

CAKE
3 cups all purpose or unbleached flour
2 cups sugar
1 cup coconut
2½ teaspoons baking soda
1 teaspoon salt
2½ teaspoons cinnamon
2 cups (4 medium) shredded carrots
1¼ cups oil
2 teaspoons vanilla
1 teaspoon grated orange peel
3 eggs
1 (11-ounce) can mandarin orange segments,
    undrained

FROSTING
3 cups powdered sugar
1 (8-ounce) package cream cheese, softened
2 tablespoons margarine or butter, melted
1 teaspoon vanilla
½ to 1 cup chopped nuts, if desired

Heat oven to 350° F. Grease 13 × 9-inch pan. Lightly spoon flour into measuring cup; level off. In large bowl, combine all cake ingredients at low speed until moistened; beat 2 minutes at high speed. Pour batter into greased pan. Bake at 350° F. for 45 to 55 minutes or until toothpick inserted in center comes out clean. Cool completely.

In large bowl, combine all frosting ingredients except nuts; beat until smooth. Spread over cooled cake; sprinkle with nuts. Store in refrigerator.

16 servings.

HIGH ALTITUDE—Above 3500 Feet: Decrease baking soda to 2 teaspoons. Bake at 350° F. for 40 to 45 minutes.

NUTRITION INFORMATION PER SERVING
SERVING SIZE: 1/16 OF RECIPE

		PERCENT U.S. RDA PER SERVING	
Calories	580	Protein	10%
Protein	6 g	Vitamin A	90%
Carbohydrate	69 g	Vitamin C	10%
Fat	31 g	Thiamine	15%
Cholesterol	55 mg	Riboflavin	10%
Sodium	390 mg	Niacin	8%
Potassium	180 mg	Calcium	4%
		Iron	10%

Pictured top to bottom: Orange-Carrot Cake, page 126; Zucchini-Date Cake

Zucchini-Date Cake

CAKE
- **1 package date bread mix**
- **½ cup sugar**
- **2 teaspoons cinnamon**
- **¾ cup oil**
- **3 eggs**
- **1½ cups shredded zucchini**

GLAZE
- **½ cup powdered sugar**
- **2 teaspoons margarine or butter, softened**
- **¼ teaspoon vanilla**
- **2 to 3 teaspoons milk or light cream**

Heat oven to 350° F. Grease and flour 9-inch square baking pan. In large bowl, combine bread mix, sugar, cinnamon, oil and eggs; mix until well blended. Stir in zucchini. Pour batter into greased and floured pan. Bake at 350° F. for 40 to 50 minutes or until toothpick inserted in center comes out clean. Cool completely.

In small bowl, combine all glaze ingredients, adding enough milk for desired consistency. Drizzle over cooled cake. Store in refrigerator. **9 to 12 servings.**

HIGH ALTITUDE—Above 3500 Feet: Add ¼ cup flour to dry bread mix. Bake as directed above.

NUTRITION INFORMATION PER SERVING
SERVING SIZE: ¹⁄₁₂ OF RECIPE

		PERCENT U.S. RDA PER SERVING	
Calories	340	Protein	6%
Protein	4 g	Vitamin A	2%
Carbohydrate	44 g	Vitamin C	*
Fat	17 g	Thiamine	8%
Cholesterol	53 mg	Riboflavin	8%
Sodium	160 mg	Niacin	4%
Potassium	115 mg	Calcium	2%
		Iron	6%

*Contains less than 2% of the U.S. RDA of this nutrient.

Pictured clockwise from left: Roast Turkey Breast with Orange Glaze, page 130; Cranberry-Orange Salad, page 130; Cauliflower and Vegetable Plate, page 131

Thanksgiving "No-Time-to-Cook" Turkey Dinner

Serves 8
Berry Sherbet Punch*
Cranberry-Orange Salad*
Warm Crescent Dinner Rolls
Roast Turkey Breast with Orange Glaze*
Pineapple-Sweet Potato Bake*
Cauliflower and Vegetable Plate*
Easy Frosty Pumpkin Pie*
Coffee   Tea
*Recipe included

*T*his festive Thanksgiving Day menu is as carefree as the name implies. If memories of past holiday dinners include days of preparation, a stovetop cluttered with saucepans, and an uncomfortably heavy dinner followed by hours of cleanup, you will welcome the differences in this contemporary alternative. Even if you must work the day before Thanksgiving, you can take your turn hosting this holiday meal with complete confidence in our step-by-step recipes and helpful timetable.

In keeping with today's trends and preferences, the menu is on the lighter side, featuring a low-fat turkey breast, fresh fruits and vegetables and a refreshing finale. Favorite flavors will evoke fond memories of traditional Thanksgivings past while streamlined additions mean minimal effort for the cook.

Shop as early as possible, saving only perishables for purchase during Thanksgiving week. You may even prefer to set your table a day or two in advance and cover it with a large sheet to keep everything sparkling. Take advantage of make-ahead suggestions for the punch, salad and pie, and of microwave directions for the vegetables. Reserve the day of the dinner solely for the final preparation steps. The result will be special-day elegance with everyday ease. You will find yourself relaxing and enjoying the holiday right along with family and guests.

Preparation Timetable

Day Before Dinner

Refrigerate cranberry juice and carbonated beverage for *Berry Sherbet Punch* • Prepare *Cranberry-Orange Salad;* refrigerate • Prepare *Easy Frosty Pumpkin Pie;* freeze.

Day of Dinner

Early in the Day: Assemble *Pineapple-Sweet Potato Bake.* Cover and refrigerate.

Several Hours Before: Prepare *Roast Turkey Breast with Orange Glaze.* Set glaze aside.

Shortly Before Serving: Unmold salad onto lettuce-lined plate; refrigerate • Bake sweet potato bake • Prepare *Cauliflower and Vegetable Plate* • Bake dinner rolls in oven when turkey breast is removed • Prepare punch • Prepare coffee and/or tea • About 15 minutes before serving dessert, remove pie from freezer to soften slightly for easier cutting.

Berry Sherbet Punch

1 quart (4 cups) cranberry juice cocktail, chilled
3½ cups orange-flavored carbonated beverage, chilled
1 pint (2 cups) raspberry sherbet

In punch bowl or large pitcher, combine cranberry juice and carbonated beverage. Scoop sherbet into mixture. Serve immediately. **9 (1-cup) servings.**

NUTRITION INFORMATION PER SERVING
SERVING SIZE: 1 CUP

		PERCENT U.S. RDA PER SERVING
Calories	170	
Protein	0 g	Protein *
Carbohydrate	41 g	Vitamin A *
Fat	1 g	Vitamin C 70%
Cholesterol	3 mg	Thiamine *
Sodium	35 mg	Riboflavin *
Potassium	65 mg	Niacin *
		Calcium 2%
		Iron *

*Contains less than 2% of the U.S. RDA of this nutrient.

Cranberry-Orange Salad

1 cup sugar
½ cup chopped walnuts
1 (12-ounce) package fresh or frozen cranberries, finely chopped
1 (11-ounce) can mandarin orange segments, drained
1 (6-ounce) package orange-flavored gelatin
2 cups boiling water
Lettuce

Oil 6-cup mold or 8 to 10 individual molds. In large bowl, combine sugar, walnuts, cranberries and oranges; set aside. In another large bowl, dissolve gelatin in boiling water. Refrigerate until slightly thickened, about 45 minutes. Stir cranberry-orange mixture into thickened gelatin. Spoon into oiled mold. Cover; refrigerate about 3 hours or until firm. To serve, unmold onto lettuce-lined serving plate or individual serving plates. Garnish as desired. **8 to 10 servings.**

NUTRITION INFORMATION PER SERVING
SERVING SIZE: ⅛ OF RECIPE

		PERCENT U.S. RDA PER SERVING
Calories	210	
Protein	3 g	Protein 4%
Carbohydrate	43 g	Vitamin A 4%
Fat	4 g	Vitamin C 20%
Cholesterol	0 mg	Thiamine 4%
Sodium	55 mg	Riboflavin *
Potassium	140 mg	Niacin *
		Calcium *
		Iron *

*Contains less than 2% of the U.S. RDA of this nutrient.

Roast Turkey Breast with Orange Glaze

2 tablespoons oil
¼ teaspoon onion powder
⅛ teaspoon garlic powder
1 (4 to 5-pound) fresh or frozen whole turkey breast, thawed
1 teaspoon dried thyme leaves
Salt and pepper

ORANGE GLAZE
1 tablespoon margarine or butter
½ cup orange marmalade
⅓ cup frozen orange juice concentrate, thawed
½ teaspoon ginger

Heat oven to 350° F. In small bowl, combine oil, onion powder and garlic powder; brush turkey breast on all sides with oil mixture. Rub thyme over all sides of turkey; sprinkle with salt and pepper. Place turkey, skin side up, on rack in roasting pan. Bake at 350° F. for 2½ to 3 hours, or until internal temperature reaches 170° F. and turkey is tender throughout.

Meanwhile, in small saucepan combine all glaze ingredients. Cook over medium heat until smooth and bubbly, stirring constantly.

Remove turkey from oven; brush with glaze. Let turkey stand 15 minutes before slicing. Pass remaining glaze to spoon over sliced turkey. **8 to 10 servings.**

NUTRITION INFORMATION PER SERVING
SERVING SIZE: ⅟₁₀ OF RECIPE

		PERCENT U.S. RDA PER SERVING
Calories	280	
Protein	43 g	Protein 70%
Carbohydrate	16 g	Vitamin A *
Fat	5 g	Vitamin C 15%
Cholesterol	117 mg	Thiamine 6%
Sodium	140 mg	Riboflavin 10%
Potassium	500 mg	Niacin 50%
		Calcium 2%
		Iron 15%

*Contains less than 2% of the U.S. RDA of this nutrient.

Pineapple-Sweet Potato Bake

1 (23-ounce) can sweet potatoes or yams, drained
3 tablespoons margarine or butter, softened
½ teaspoon salt
1 (8-ounce) can crushed pineapple, drained
⅓ cup orange juice
¼ cup firmly packed brown sugar
¼ cup chopped pecans

Heat oven to 350° F. Grease 1-quart casserole. In medium bowl, mash sweet potatoes with margarine and salt. Add pineapple and orange juice; blend well. Spoon into greased casserole; sprinkle with brown sugar and pecans. Bake at 350° F. for 25 to 30 minutes or until thoroughly heated.

6 to 8 servings.

MICROWAVE DIRECTIONS: Prepare casserole mixture as directed above; spoon into 1-quart microwave-safe casserole. Microwave on HIGH for 5 to 7 minutes or until thoroughly heated, rotating casserole ½ turn halfway through cooking.

NUTRITION INFORMATION PER SERVING

SERVING SIZE: ⅛ OF RECIPE		PERCENT U.S. RDA PER SERVING	
Calories	190	Protein	2%
Protein	2 g	Vitamin A	120%
Carbohydrate	31 g	Vitamin C	15%
Fat	7 g	Thiamine	4%
Cholesterol	0 mg	Riboflavin	2%
Sodium	220 mg	Niacin	2%
Potassium	250 mg	Calcium	2%
		Iron	6%

until cauliflower is tender. Set aside. Place broccoli-carrot mixture in 1-quart microwave-safe casserole; cover with microwave-safe plastic wrap. Microwave on HIGH for 6 to 9 minutes or until thoroughly heated, rotating ½ turn halfway through cooking; drain. Remove plastic wrap from cauliflower; place in center of large serving plate. Arrange broccoli-carrot mixture around cauliflower. Spoon sauce over cauliflower.* Serve any additional sauce on the side.

TIP: *If vegetables become cold after sauce has been added, the entire vegetable platter can be reheated. Microwave on HIGH for 3 to 4 minutes, rotating ½ turn after 2 minutes of cooking.

NUTRITION INFORMATION PER SERVING

SERVING SIZE: ⅛ OF RECIPE		PERCENT U.S. RDA PER SERVING	
Calories	170	Protein	4%
Protein	3 g	Vitamin A	30%
Carbohydrate	7 g	Vitamin C	50%
Fat	14 g	Thiamine	4%
Cholesterol	15 mg	Riboflavin	2%
Sodium	260 mg	Niacin	2%
Potassium	300 mg	Calcium	4%
		Iron	2%

Cauliflower and Vegetable Plate

½ cup mayonnaise
½ cup dairy sour cream
½ teaspoon dried dill weed
1 teaspoon prepared mustard
½ teaspoon lemon juice
1 cup water
½ teaspoon salt
1 medium head cauliflower, leaves removed, stem trimmed
1 (16-ounce) package frozen broccoli, carrots, water chestnuts and red peppers

In small bowl, combine mayonnaise, sour cream, dill weed, mustard and lemon juice; blend well. Set aside.

In large saucepan, bring water and salt to a boil. Add cauliflower; reduce heat. Cover and simmer until tender, about 15 to 20 minutes. Meanwhile, cook broccoli-carrot mixture as directed on package; drain. Place cauliflower in center of large platter; arrange broccoli-carrot mixture around cauliflower. Spoon sauce over cauliflower. Serve any additional sauce on the side.

8 servings.

MICROWAVE DIRECTIONS: In small bowl, combine mayonnaise, sour cream, dill weed, mustard and lemon juice; blend well. Set aside.

Wrap cauliflower loosely in microwave-safe plastic wrap. Microwave on HIGH for 5 to 7 minutes or

Easy Frosty Pumpkin Pie

CRUST
¼ cup margarine or butter
1½ cups crushed gingersnap cookies

FILLING
1 (16-ounce) can (2 cups) pumpkin
1 pint (2 cups) vanilla ice cream, softened
1 cup powdered sugar
1½ teaspoons pumpkin pie spice
⅛ teaspoons salt
1 teaspoon vanilla
2 cups frozen whipped topping, thawed

In small saucepan, melt margarine. Remove from heat; stir in crushed cookies. Press mixture evenly in bottom and up sides of 9-inch pie pan; refrigerate.

In large bowl, combine all filling ingredients except whipped topping; blend until smooth. Fold whipped topping into pumpkin mixture. Pour into prepared crust. Freeze several hours or until firm. Let stand at room temperature at least 15 minutes before serving. Garnish as desired.

8 to 10 servings.

NUTRITION INFORMATION PER SERVING

SERVING SIZE: 1/10 OF RECIPE		PERCENT U.S. RDA PER SERVING	
Calories	280	Protein	4%
Protein	3 g	Vitamin A	210%
Carbohydrate	37 g	Vitamin C	2%
Fat	13 g	Thiamine	4%
Cholesterol	19 mg	Riboflavin	6%
Sodium	210 mg	Niacin	2%
Potassium	230 mg	Calcium	6%
		Iron	6%

Pictured clockwise from left: Fruit 'n Spinach Salad, page 134; Hanukkah Cutouts, page 135; Potato Pancakes, page 135; Applesauce, page 135

Hanukkah Supper

Serves 6 to 8
Chilled Fruit Juices
Pomegranate and Greens Salad*
or
Fruit 'n Spinach Salad*
Savory Baked Chicken*
Potato Pancakes*   Applesauce*
Raspberry-Filled Jelly Doughnuts*
and/or
Hanukkah Cutouts*
Coffee   Tea
*Recipe included

One of the highlights of the Jewish calendar is Hanukkah, often called the Festival of Lights. Usually falling in December and lasting eight days, it is a time for family gatherings, gift exchanges and the all-important symbolic lighting of the menorah. This eight-branched candelabrum is the centerpiece of the celebration, serving as a reminder of a miraculous event centuries ago when a one-day supply of oil was able to keep temple lights burning for eight days.

Traditional Hanukkah colors of blue and white are accented in table appointments, other decorations, gift wrap, and icing on special cookies.

Although celebratory menus vary, most families prefer heritage foods. One staple is latkes, or fried potato pancakes. Frequently the pancakes are served with applesauce, a colorful salad and an entree of baked chicken, beef brisket or salmon. A perfect alternative for Savory Baked Chicken is the salmon steaks served with slices of lemon in place of the spinach sauce from our Father's Day Dinner menu on page 114. Jelly doughnuts, a traditional ending to the Hanukkah meal, which are usually made from scratch and fried, can now be baked as we have done in Raspberry-Filled Jelly Doughnuts. The children will enjoy helping with these because they are so easy and there is no danger of being burned by hot fat. Cutting the cookies in symbolic shapes and then decorating offer another opportunity for family togetherness—a cornerstone of this cherished holiday.

Preparation Timetable

Day Before Supper

Refrigerate fruit juices • Prepare *Hanukkah Cutouts* • Wash greens for *Pomegranate and Greens Salad* or *Fruit 'n Spinach Salad;* place in plastic bags and refrigerate • Prepare *Applesauce;* cover and refrigerate.

Day of Supper

Early in the Day: Section and slice fruit for fruit salad; place in container and refrigerate • Prepare dressing for salad; cover and refrigerate • Clean chicken for *Savory Baked Chicken;* cover and refrigerate • Prepare *Raspberry-Filled Jelly Doughnuts.*

Before Serving: Prepare baked chicken • Prepare coffee and/or tea • Toss or arrange salads • Prepare *Potato Pancakes.*

Pomegranate and Greens Salad

DRESSING
- ¼ cup sugar
- ½ teaspoon salt
- ¼ teaspoon white pepper
- 1 garlic clove, minced
- ¼ cup raspberry or white wine vinegar
- 2 tablespoons olive or vegetable oil

SALAD
- 6 cups torn fresh spinach
- 3 cups torn leaf lettuce
- 3 cups torn iceberg lettuce
- ½ cup pomegranate seeds

In small bowl or jar with tight-fitting lid, combine all dressing ingredients; mix well. Refrigerate.

Just before serving, combine all salad ingredients in large salad bowl. Stir dressing; pour over salad. Toss gently to coat greens.
6 to 8 servings.

NUTRITION INFORMATION PER SERVING
SERVING SIZE: ⅛ OF RECIPE

		PERCENT U.S. RDA PER SERVING	
Calories	90	Protein	2%
Protein	2 g	Vitamin A	70%
Carbohydrate	11 g	Vitamin C	30%
Fat	4 g	Thiamine	2%
Cholesterol	0 mg	Riboflavin	6%
Sodium	170 mg	Niacin	2%
Potassium	350 mg	Calcium	6%
		Iron	8%

Fruit 'n Spinach Salad

CITRUS-HONEY DRESSING
- ¼ cup orange or lemon juice
- 2 tablespoons oil
- 2 tablespoons honey

SALAD
- 8 cups torn fresh spinach
- 2 cups red grapefruit sections
- 2 cups orange sections
- 2 cups diagonally sliced bananas
- 2 kiwifruit, peeled, sliced

In jar with tight-fitting lid, combine all dressing ingredients; shake well. Refrigerate at least 30 minutes to blend flavors.

Divide spinach among 8 salad plates. Arrange fruit over spinach; drizzle with dressing.
8 servings.

NUTRITION INFORMATION PER SERVING
SERVING SIZE: ⅛ OF RECIPE

		PERCENT U.S. RDA PER SERVING	
Calories	160	Protein	4%
Protein	3 g	Vitamin A	80%
Carbohydrate	28 g	Vitamin C	140%
Fat	4 g	Thiamine	8%
Cholesterol	0 mg	Riboflavin	10%
Sodium	45 mg	Niacin	4%
Potassium	700 mg	Calcium	8%
		Iron	10%

Savory Baked Chicken

- 2 (2½ to 3-pounds) frying chickens, cut up
- ⅓ cup margarine or butter, melted
- 2 tablespoons lemon juice
- ½ teaspoon salt
- ½ teaspoon dried tarragon leaves
- ½ teaspoon paprika
- ¼ teaspoon pepper

Heat oven to 325° F. Place chicken pieces in 2 ungreased 13 × 9-inch pans. In small bowl, combine margarine and lemon juice; mix well. Pour over chicken. Sprinkle with salt, tarragon, paprika and pepper. Cover with foil. Bake at 325° F. for 45 minutes. Uncover; bake an additional 15 minutes or until tender. **8 servings.**

NUTRITION INFORMATION PER SERVING
SERVING SIZE: ⅛ OF RECIPE

		PERCENT U.S. RDA PER SERVING	
Calories	280	Protein	50%
Protein	32 g	Vitamin A	8%
Carbohydrate	0 g	Vitamin C	*
Fat	16 g	Thiamine	4%
Cholesterol	97 mg	Riboflavin	10%
Sodium	320 mg	Niacin	50%
Potassium	280 mg	Calcium	2%
		Iron	8%

*Contains less than 2% of the U.S. RDA of this nutrient.

Raspberry-Filled Jelly Doughnuts

- 6 tablespoons margarine or butter, melted
- ¾ cup sugar
- ¾ teaspoon cinnamon
- ⅓ cup raspberry jelly
- 1 (10-ounce) can refrigerated buttermilk *fluffy* biscuits

Heat oven to 375° F. Place melted margarine in small bowl. In another small bowl, combine sugar and cinnamon; set aside. Stir jelly until smooth. Seal tip of large baster with foil. Remove rubber bulb. Spoon jelly into baster; replace bulb.

Prepare and bake biscuits according to package directions. Immediately dip each hot biscuit into melted margarine, coating all sides. Roll in sugar mixture, heavily coating all sides of each biscuit. Remove foil from tip of baster. Insert baster in side of each biscuit; squeeze small amount of jelly in center. (Refill as needed.) Serve warm or cold.
10 doughnuts.

NUTRITION INFORMATION PER SERVING
SERVING SIZE: 1 DOUGHNUT

		PERCENT U.S. RDA PER SERVING	
Calories	240	Protein	2%
Protein	2 g	Vitamin A	6%
Carbohydrate	34 g	Vitamin C	*
Fat	11 g	Thiamine	6%
Cholesterol	2 mg	Riboflavin	4%
Sodium	370 mg	Niacin	4%
Potassium	30 mg	Calcium	*
		Iron	4%

*Contains less than 2% of the U.S. RDA of this nutrient.

Potato Pancakes

6 cups shredded, peeled potatoes*
1 cup finely chopped onion
¼ cup flour
6 eggs, beaten
2 teaspoons salt
¼ teaspoon pepper
   Oil

Place shredded potatoes in a clean cloth; squeeze to remove excess moisture. In medium bowl, combine potatoes and all remaining ingredients except oil.

Heat ¼ inch oil in heavy skillet over medium heat. Using about ⅓ cup potato mixture for each, form very thin pancake patties 3 to 4 inches in diameter. Fry 2 to 3 minutes on each side or until lightly browned. Drain on paper towels. Add additional oil to skillet if needed to fry remaining pancakes. Serve immediately with Applesauce (below).

16 pancakes.

TIP: *Shred potatoes into cold water to prevent darkening; drain well.

NUTRITION INFORMATION PER SERVING
SERVING SIZE: 1
PANCAKE

		PERCENT U.S. RDA PER SERVING	
Calories	180	Protein	6%
Protein	4 g	Vitamin A	2%
Carbohydrate	13 g	Vitamin C	20%
Fat	12 g	Thiamine	4%
Cholesterol	80 mg	Riboflavin	6%
Sodium	290 mg	Niacin	4%
Potassium	350 mg	Calcium	*
		Iron	4%

*Contains less than 2% of the U.S. RDA of this nutrient.

Applesauce

6 to 8 medium apples, peeled, quartered
½ cup water
½ to ¾ cup sugar or brown sugar
1 to 2 tablespoons red cinnamon candies

In large saucepan, combine apples and water. Bring to a boil. Cover; simmer over low heat 15 to 20 minutes or until tender, stirring occasionally. Stir in sugar and cinnamon candies; cook until thoroughly heated.

8 (½-cup) servings.

NUTRITION INFORMATION PER SERVING
SERVING SIZE: ½ CUP

		PERCENT U.S. RDA PER SERVING	
Calories	160	Protein	*
Protein	0 g	Vitamin A	*
Carbohydrate	41 g	Vitamin C	6%
Fat	0 g	Thiamine	*
Cholesterol	0 mg	Riboflavin	*
Sodium	10 mg	Niacin	*
Potassium	150 mg	Calcium	*
		Iron	*

*Contains less than 2% of the U.S. RDA of this nutrient.

Hanukkah Cutouts

1¼ cups powdered sugar
1 cup margarine or butter, softened
1 teaspoon vanilla
1 egg
2½ cups all purpose or unbleached flour
1 teaspoon baking soda
1 teaspoon cream of tartar

FROSTING
1½ cups powdered sugar
3–4 tablespoons milk

DECORATOR FROSTING
1 cup powdered sugar
1½ teaspoons margarine or butter, softened
   Blue food coloring
1–2 tablespoons milk

In large bowl, beat powdered sugar and margarine until light and fluffy. Add vanilla and egg; blend well. Lightly spoon flour into measuring cup; level off. Stir in flour, baking soda and cream of tartar; mix well. Cover with plastic wrap; refrigerate 1 hour for easier handling.

Heat oven to 375° F. On lightly floured surface, roll out dough, ⅓ at a time, to ⅛-inch thickness. Refrigerate remaining dough. Cut out cookies with lightly floured cookie cutters. Place 1 inch apart on ungreased cookie sheets. Bake at 375° F. for 6 to 9 minutes or until edges are light golden brown. Immediately remove from cookie sheets. Cool completely.

In small bowl, combine all frosting ingredients, adding milk until mixture is of thin spreading consistency; blend until smooth. Frost cooled cookies. Allow frosting to set before decorating.

In another small bowl, combine all decorator frosting ingredients; blend until mixture is of desired consistency for piping. With pastry bag and writing tip, decorate cookies as desired.

5 dozen cookies.

HIGH ALTITUDE—Above 3500 Feet: Decrease powdered sugar to 1 cup.

NUTRITION INFORMATION PER SERVING
SERVING SIZE: 1
COOKIE

		PERCENT U.S. RDA PER SERVING	
Calories	60	Protein	*
Protein	1 g	Vitamin A	2%
Carbohydrate	6 g	Vitamin C	*
Fat	3 g	Thiamine	2%
Cholesterol	4 mg	Riboflavin	*
Sodium	55 mg	Niacin	*
Potassium	10 mg	Calcium	*
		Iron	*

*Contains less than 2% of the U.S. RDA of this nutrient.

Pictured from top: Broccoli Spears with Lime Butter, page 138; Savory Fruit Stuffing, page 139; Honey-Glazed Cornish Hens, page 139

Christmas Dinner

Serves 8
Berry Wine Sparkler*
Cream of Walnut Soup*
Home-Style Crisp Tossed Salad*
Onion Finger Rolls*
Honey-Glazed Cornish Hens*
Savory Fruit Stuffing*
Broccoli Spears with Lime Butter*
Flaming Bananas and Ice Cream*
Coffee   Tea
*Recipe included

---

*H*oliday hosting can be pure pleasure or a frenetic, burdensome experience. We opt for the first with a festive and hassle-free menu. We admit it can be easy to lose sight of the true Christmas spirit during this fast-paced season. But with a little preplanning and uncomplicated, yet impressive fare, you can enjoy opening your home to family and friends even at this busy time.

In addition to easy-to-follow instructions that bring superb results, this menu solves the problem of what to do with endless leftovers from a large ham, roast or turkey. With one golden Honey-Glazed Cornish Hen per person, presentation is picture-perfect and every bite is enjoyed in one sitting. Another bonus? The hens are the only items requiring oven space. The rolls and soup are definite make-aheads. Just add the half-and-half to the soup during the reheating step. If you have holiday cookies on hand, show them off on a pretty platter to embellish the glamorous flaming dessert.

Almost everyone agrees—the most appreciated gifts are homemade. Consider this holiday dinner a very special gift only you can present to family or friends. Your culinary efforts will reap great dividends in terms of savoring this special season.

Preparation Timetable

Several Days Ahead
Prepare *Onion Finger Rolls;* cool completely, wrap in foil and freeze.

Day Before Dinner
Clean and prepare greens and vegetables for *Home-Style Crisp Tossed Salad;* place in plastic bags and refrigerate • Prepare dressing for salad; refrigerate • Clean hens for *Honey-Glazed Cornish Hens;* cover and refrigerate • Refrigerate wine and raspberry-cranberry drink for *Berry Wine Sparkler.*

Day of Dinner
Early in the Day: Remove rolls from freezer • Prepare *Cream of Walnut Soup,* omitting half-and-half; pour into nonmetal container and refrigerate.

Several Hours Before: Toast almonds and measure out ingredients for *Flaming Bananas and Ice Cream.* Do not peel and slice bananas until ready to serve • Prepare *Savory Fruit Stuffing* • Complete preparation of hens.

Shortly Before Serving: Reheat soup over low heat; stir in half-and-half • Prepare salad • Warm foil-wrapped rolls • Prepare *Broccoli Spears with Lime Butter* • Prepare coffee and/or tea and wine sparkler • When ready to serve dessert, complete preparation of bananas and ice cream.

Berry Wine Sparkler

1 (750-milliliter) bottle white sparkling wine, chilled
4 cups raspberry-cranberry drink, chilled

In 2-quart nonmetal pitcher, combine wine and juice; stir gently. Serve immediately.
8 (¾-cup) servings.

NUTRITION INFORMATION PER SERVING
SERVING SIZE: ¾ CUP

		PERCENT U.S. RDA PER SERVING	
Calories	140	Protein	*
Protein	0 g	Vitamin A	*
Carbohydrate	19 g	Vitamin C	70%
Fat	0 g	Thiamine	*
Cholesterol	0 mg	Riboflavin	*
Sodium	10 mg	Niacin	*
Potassium	100 mg	Calcium	*
		Iron	*

*Contains less than 2% of the U.S. RDA of this nutrient.

Cream of Walnut Soup

3 cups chicken broth
1 cup finely chopped walnuts
2 tablespoons finely chopped celery
2 tablespoons finely chopped onion
⅛ teaspoon nutmeg
2 tablespoons margarine or butter
2 tablespoons flour
½ cup milk
1 cup half-and-half
Fresh parsley sprigs
Walnut pieces

In large saucepan, combine chicken broth, walnuts, celery, onion and nutmeg. Bring to a boil; reduce heat. Cover; simmer 30 minutes.

In blender container or food processor bowl with metal blade, puree broth mixture; strain, if desired. Return to saucepan.

Melt margarine in small saucepan over medium heat; stir in flour. Cook until smooth and bubbly. Gradually stir in milk. Cook until mixture boils and thickens, stirring constantly. Gradually stir into broth mixture; simmer over low heat for 5 minutes, stirring occasionally. Stir in half-and-half. Heat gently, stirring frequently; do not boil. Garnish with parsley sprigs and walnut pieces.
8 (½-cup) servings.

NUTRITION INFORMATION PER SERVING
SERVING SIZE: ½ CUP

		PERCENT U.S. RDA PER SERVING	
Calories	200	Protein	4%
Protein	3 g	Vitamin A	10%
Carbohydrate	20 g	Vitamin C	*
Fat	12 g	Thiamine	4%
Cholesterol	1 mg	Riboflavin	4%
Sodium	280 mg	Niacin	4%
Potassium	130 mg	Calcium	2%
		Iron	4%

*Contains less than 2% of the U.S. RDA of this nutrient.

Home-Style Crisp Tossed Salad

4 cups torn romaine or other crisp lettuce leaves
1½ cups thinly sliced celery
1 cup shredded green or red cabbage
½ cup thinly sliced carrots
½ cup thinly sliced radishes
2 to 3 tablespoons thinly sliced green onions

DRESSING
⅓ cup sugar
½ teaspoon seasoned salt
¼ teaspoon celery seed
2 to 3 tablespoons cider or wine vinegar

In large bowl, combine all vegetables. In small bowl or jar with tight-fitting lid, combine all dressing ingredients; mix well. Pour dressing over vegetables; toss well. Serve immediately.
8 (1-cup) servings.

NUTRITION INFORMATION PER SERVING
SERVING SIZE: 1 CUP

		PERCENT U.S. RDA PER SERVING	
Calories	50	Protein	*
Protein	1 g	Vitamin A	60%
Carbohydrate	12 g	Vitamin C	25%
Fat	0 g	Thiamine	2%
Cholesterol	0 mg	Riboflavin	2%
Sodium	130 mg	Niacin	*
Potassium	220 mg	Calcium	2%
		Iron	2%

*Contains less than 2% of the U.S. RDA of this nutrient.

Broccoli Spears with Lime Butter

1 (16-ounce) package frozen broccoli spears
3 tablespoons butter or margarine
1 tablespoon lime juice
¼ teaspoon salt
Dash pepper

Cook broccoli according to package directions; drain. Place in serving dish. In small saucepan, melt butter; stir in lime juice. Pour over broccoli spears; season with salt and pepper.
8 servings.

NUTRITION INFORMATION PER SERVING
SERVING SIZE: ⅛ OF RECIPE

		PERCENT U.S. RDA PER SERVING	
Calories	50	Protein	2%
Protein	1 g	Vitamin A	10%
Carbohydrate	3 g	Vitamin C	30%
Fat	4 g	Thiamine	*
Cholesterol	12 mg	Riboflavin	2%
Sodium	120 mg	Niacin	*
Potassium	135 mg	Calcium	2%
		Iron	2%

*Contains less than 2% of the U.S. RDA of this nutrient.

Honey-Glazed Cornish Hens

8 (1 to 1½-lb.) Cornish game hens*
Salt and pepper
Savory Fruit Stuffing
¼ cup margarine or butter, melted
2 tablespoons honey

Heat oven to 350° F. Remove giblets. Rinse hens; pat dry. Sprinkle cavities with salt and pepper. Lightly stuff each with ½ cup Savory Fruit Stuffing. Tie legs together with string. Place hens in ungreased 15 × 10 × 1-inch baking pan. In small bowl, combine margarine and honey; brush hens with honey mixture. Bake at 350° F. for 1¼ hours or until hens are fork-tender and juices run clear. Remove strings before serving.
8 servings.

TIP: *If smaller servings are desired, use 4 hens that have been split in half. Place split hens skin side up on top of stuffing; brush with honey mixture. Bake at 350° F. for 1 hour or until tender.

NUTRITION INFORMATION PER SERVING

SERVING SIZE: ⅛ OF RECIPE		PERCENT U.S. RDA PER SERVING	
Calories	670	Protein	100%
Protein	66 g	Vitamin A	20%
Carbohydrate	25 g	Vitamin C	*
Fat	34 g	Thiamine	15%
Cholesterol	196 mg	Riboflavin	25%
Sodium	600 mg	Niacin	110%
Potassium	670 mg	Calcium	6%
		Iron	20%

*Contains less than 2% of the U.S. RDA of this nutrient.

Savory Fruit Stuffing

½ cup margarine or butter
¼ cup chopped celery
¼ cup chopped onion
⅛ teaspoon allspice
4 cups dry bread cubes
½ cup dried fruit bits
½ cup water

Melt margarine in large skillet or saucepan over medium-high heat. Stir in celery, onion and allspice; cook and stir until vegetables are tender. Stir in remaining ingredients; cook until thoroughly heated.
8 (½-cup) servings.

NUTRITION INFORMATION PER SERVING

SERVING SIZE: ¼ CUP		PERCENT U.S. RDA PER SERVING	
Calories	200	Protein	4%
Protein	3 g	Vitamin A	10%
Carbohydrate	20 g	Vitamin C	*
Fat	12 g	Thiamine	4%
Cholesterol	1 mg	Riboflavin	4%
Sodium	280 mg	Niacin	4%
Potassium	130 mg	Calcium	2%
		Iron	4%

*Contains less than 2% of the U.S. RDA of this nutrient.

Onion Finger Rolls

1 package hot roll mix
1 tablespoon instant minced onion
1 cup water heated to 120 to 130° F.
2 tablespoons margarine or butter, softened
1 egg
2 tablespoons margarine or butter, melted
¼ to ½ teaspoon onion powder

Grease 2 cookie sheets. In large bowl, combine flour mixture from package with yeast from foil packet and minced onion; blend well. Stir in *hot* water, 2 tablespoons margarine and egg until dough pulls away from sides of bowl. Turn dough out onto lightly floured surface. With greased or floured hands, shape dough into a ball. Knead dough for 5 minutes until smooth. Cover with large bowl; let rest 5 minutes.

On lightly floured surface, roll dough to 12 × 9-inch rectangle. With sharp knife, cut 4 equal strips crosswise; cut 9 strips lengthwise, forming 36 (3 × 1-inch) finger rolls. Place rolls on greased cookie sheets. Brush tops of rolls with 2 tablespoons melted margarine; sprinkle with onion powder. Cover loosely with greased plastic wrap and cloth towel. Let rise in warm place (80 to 85° F.) 30 minutes.

Heat oven to 375° F. Uncover dough. Bake at 375° F. for 12 to 15 minutes or until light golden brown. Remove from cookie sheets; cool completely on wire racks or serve warm.
36 rolls.

HIGH ALTITUDE—Above 3500 Feet: No change.

NUTRITION INFORMATION PER SERVING

SERVING SIZE: 1 ROLL		PERCENT U.S. RDA PER SERVING	
Calories	60	Protein	2%
Protein	2 g	Vitamin A	*
Carbohydrate	9 g	Vitamin C	*
Fat	2 g	Thiamine	6%
Cholesterol	6 mg	Riboflavin	4%
Sodium	105 mg	Niacin	4%
Potassium	20 mg	Calcium	*
		Iron	2%

*Contains less than 2% of the U.S. RDA of this nutrient.

Flaming Bananas and Ice Cream

Flaming Bananas and Ice Cream

2 tablespoons sliced almonds
¾ cup firmly packed brown sugar
  Dash nutmeg
3 tablespoons butter or margarine
¼ cup rum*
4 firm medium bananas, cut in half lengthwise
  and crosswise
¼ cup golden raisins
2 tablespoons rum, if desired*
1 quart (4 cups) vanilla ice cream

In large skillet over medium-high heat, toast almonds until golden brown, stirring constantly. Reduce heat to medium-low; stir in brown sugar, nutmeg and butter until melted and well combined. Add ¼ cup rum, bananas and raisins; simmer for 5 minutes, stirring gently. Place in chafing dish, if desired.

In small saucepan over low heat, warm 2 tablespoons rum; ignite and pour slowly over banana mixture, stirring until flames disappear. Serve sauce over ice cream.
8 servings.

TIP: *One-fourth cup water and ¼ to ½ teaspoon rum extract can be substituted for ¼ cup rum. The 2 tablespoons rum for flaming can be omitted.

NUTRITION INFORMATION PER SERVING

SERVING SIZE: ⅛ OF RECIPE		PERCENT U.S. RDA PER SERVING	
Calories	350	Protein	4%
Protein	4 g	Vitamin A	10%
Carbohydrate	54 g	Vitamin C	6%
Fat	13 g	Thiamine	4%
Cholesterol	41 mg	Riboflavin	15%
Sodium	110 mg	Niacin	2%
Potassium	480 mg	Calcium	10%
		Iron	6%

Appendix

Pillsbury Products Used

DRY GROCERY PRODUCTS:

Canned Vegetables
B in B® Brand Sliced Mushrooms
Green Giant® Mexicorn® Whole Kernel Golden
  Sweet Corn with Red and Green Sweet Peppers
Green Giant® Mushrooms Pieces and Stems
Green Giant® Sliced Mushrooms
Green Giant® Valley Combinations® Frozen Broccoli
  Carrot Fanfare
Green Giant® Whole Mushrooms
Joan of Arc® or Green Giant® Great Northern Beans
Joan of Arc® or Green Giant® Kidney Beans
Joan of Arc® or Green Giant® Pork & Beans

Flour
Pillsbury's BEST® All Purpose Flour
Pillsbury's BEST® Unbleached All Purpose Flour
Pillsbury's BEST® Whole Wheat Flour

Cake Mixes and Frosting
Pillsbury Plus® Devil's Food Cake Mix
Pillsbury Plus® Funfetti® Cake Mix
Pillsbury Plus® Lemon Cake Mix
Pillsbury Plus® White Cake Mix
Pillsbury Plus® Yellow Cake Mix
Pillsbury Vanilla Frosting Supreme™

Specialty
Hungry Jack® Mashed Potato Flakes
Pillsbury Banana Quick Bread Mix
Pillsbury Date Quick Bread Mix
Pillsbury Fudge Brownie Mix
Pillsbury Hot Roll Mix
Pillsbury Nut Quick Bread Mix

REFRIGERATED PRODUCTS:

Hungry Jack® Refrigerated Buttermilk Fluffy Biscuits
Pillsbury All Ready Pie Crusts
Pillsbury All Ready Pizza Crust
Pillsbury Refrigerated Biscuits
Pillsbury Refrigerated Crusty French Loaf
Pillsbury Refrigerated Quick Crescent Dinner Rolls
Pillsbury Refrigerated Soft Breadsticks
Pillsbury's BEST® Refrigerated Chocolate Chip
  Cookies
Pillsbury's BEST® Refrigerated Sugar Cookies

FROZEN PRODUCTS:

Green Giant® Frozen Broccoli Spears
Green Giant® Frozen Cut Green Beans
Green Giant® Frozen Sweet Peas
Green Giant® Harvest Fresh® Frozen Baby Early
  Peas
Green Giant® Harvest Fresh® Frozen Chopped
  Spinach
Green Giant® Harvest Fresh® Frozen Cut Broccoli
Green Giant® Niblet Ears® Frozen Corn-on-the-Cob
Green Giant® Rice Originals® Frozen Rice Medley

Nutrition Information

Nutrition Information: Pillsbury recipe analysis is provided per serving or per unit of food and is based on the most current nutritional values available from the United States Department of Agriculture (USDA) and food manufacturers. Each recipe is calculated for number of calories; grams of protein, carbohydrate and fat; and milligrams of cholesterol, sodium and potassium.

Vitamin and mineral levels are stated as percentages of United States Recommended Daily Allowances. RDAs are the dietary standards determined by the U.S. Food and Drug Administration for healthy people. If you are following a medically prescribed diet, consult your physician or registered dietitian about using this nutrition information.

Calculating Nutrition Information: Recipe analysis is calculated on:

• A single serving based on the largest number of servings, or on a specific amount (1 tablespoon) or unit (1 cookie).

• The first ingredient or amount when more than one is listed.

• "If desired" or garnishing ingredients when they are included in the ingredient listing.

• Only the amount of a marinade or frying oil absorbed during preparation.

Using Nutrition Information: The amount of nutrients a person needs is determined by one's age, size and activity level. The following are general guidelines you can use for evaluating your daily food intake:

Calories: 2,350
Protein: 45 to 65 grams
Carbohydrates: 340 grams
Fat: 80 grams or less
Cholesterol: 300 milligrams or less
Sodium: 2,400 milligrams

A nutritionally balanced diet recommends limiting intake of fat to 30 percent or less of total daily calories. One gram of fat is 9 calories. You can determine the fat content of recipes or products with the following formula:

$$\frac{\text{GRAMS OF FAT PER SERVING} \times 9}{\text{TOTAL CALORIES PER SERVING}} = \begin{array}{c}\text{PERCENT}\\\text{OF CALORIES}\\\text{FROM FAT}\end{array}$$

$$\left(\text{Ex. } \frac{8 \times 9}{310} = \frac{72}{310} = 22\%\right)$$

Index